THE MULTIPLE STAGE IN SPAIN DURING THE FIFTEENTH AND SIXTEENTH CENTURIES

THE MULTIPLE STAGE IN SPAIN DURING THE FIFTEENTH AND SIXTEENTH CENTURIES

A DISSERTATION PRESENTED TO THE
FACULTY OF PRINCETON UNIVER-
SITY IN CANDIDACY FOR THE DE-
GREE OF DOCTOR OF PHILOSOPHY

BY

WILLIAM HUTCHINSON SHOEMAKER
Princeton University

GREENWOOD PRESS, PUBLISHERS
WESTPORT, CONNECTICUT

Library of Congress Cataloging in Publication Data

Shoemaker, William Hutchinson, 1902-
   The multiple stage in Spain during the fifteenth and
sixteenth centuries.

   Reprint of the 1935 ed.
   Originally presented as the author's thesis,
Princeton, 1933.
   Bibliography: p.
   1.   Theaters--Spain--Stage-setting and scenery.
2.   Spanish drama--Early to 1500--History and criticism.
3.   Spanish drama--Classical period, 1500-1700--
History and criticism.   I.   Title.
PN2087.S7S5   1973   792'.0946   78-137076
ISBN 0-8371-5539-8

Recommended by the
Department of Modern Languages and Literatures
for Acceptance September, 1933

Originally published in 1935 by Princeton University Press,
Princeton New Jersey

Reprinted by arrangement with Princeton University Press

Reprinted from an original copy in the collections of the
University of Illinois Library

Reprinted in 1973 by Greenwood Press,
a division of Congressional Information Service, Inc.
88 Post Road West, Westport, Connecticut 06881

Library of Congress catalog card number 78-137076
ISBN 0-8371-5539-8

Printed in the United States of America

10 9 8 7 6 5 4 3

TO
the memory of
one who for six years as teacher, coun-
sellor and friend guided my studies in
the language and literature of Spain

CHARLES CARROLL MARDEN

FOREWORD

It is with deep appreciation that I wish to express my gratitude to Professor Joseph E. Gillet of Bryn Mawr College, sometime Visiting Professor at Princeton University, under whose kind and scholarly supervision this monograph was prepared, and to Professors Donald Clive Stuart and F. Courtney Tarr of Princeton University for their generous and helpful criticism at various stages of its development.

A Note on Abbreviations

Besides those in general use (e.g., p. = page), the following abbreviations are used:

(1) SD=stage direction.

(2) An Arabic numeral alone which refers to a dramatic text indicates the line of text so numbered (e.g., 128=line 128).

(3) Wherever possible, references to periodicals follow the system adopted by the *Revista de filología española (RFE)*.

TABLE OF CONTENTS

INTRODUCTION

No systematic study of the methods of staging plays in the Iberian Peninsula before Lope de Vega has yet been attempted. Professor Buchanan's article on the Madrid *corrales*[1] makes no attempt to suggest what the earlier theater might have been. Rennert's *The Spanish Stage*[2] remains the only extensive treatment of the external and material side of the drama. In this book, however, the theater prior to Lope de Vega is dismissed with some interesting but unconnected items in a few pages of the first two chapters. In the standard histories of the Spanish drama mention of staging methods is incidental, although lengthy references to early practices sometimes appear as in the works of Schack,[2] Milá y Fontanals,[2] Mérimée,[2] Bonilla[2] and Crawford.[2] Several important compilations of material on the drama like the various *Anales* of Sánchez-Arjona,[2] Alonso Cortés,[2] and Díaz de Escovar,[2] the *Apuntes* of Fernández Duro,[2] and the *Nuevos datos* of Pérez Pastor[2] contain extremely valuable data arranged in chronological order. But in none of these works have the scanty miscellaneous facts been adequately analyzed or properly correlated and interpreted. In fact, no study has brought to light the plans and methods by which fifteenth and sixteenth century plays were performed.

Any study of early staging methods in Spain is fraught with serious difficulties, some of which are attributable, as Manuel Cañete observed,[3] to unwarranted generalizations based on the statements of contemporary writers. Cervantes,[4] Agustín de Rojas[5] and Juan Rufo[6] are in agreement. All three speak of the meagerness of costumes and properties and the poverty of scenery on the sixteenth century stage. Their remarks refer specifically, however, to the theater of travelling or "barnstorming" troupes of actors

---

[1] "At a Spanish Theater in the Seventeenth Century." See Bibliography.
[2] See Bibliography for full titles of all works referred to in this study.
[3] *Teatro español del siglo XVI*, 323.
[4] "Prólogo al lector" (which prefaced the publication of his *Comedias y entremeses* in 1615), 6-7.
[5] *El viaje entretenido* (1603), in *NBAE*, XXI, 488-490; 493-497 (Loa de la comedia).
[6] *Alabanças de la comedia* (1596), 605 n. 1.

like those of Lope de Rueda and his successors. The company of
Angulo el Malo must have been such a troupe, for when Don
Quixote met them, they were on their way from one village to another to give a second performance that day of the "auto de las
Cortes de la Muerte."[7] Cervantes, Rojas and Rufo refer neither
to the churches, to the great halls of private palaces, nor even to
outdoor stages more elaborate than those used by the travelling
companies. Any extension of their remarks to these other stages
is therefore without foundation and decidedly misleading. Their
remarks constitute, at best, a one-sided and partial picture of the
Spanish stage in the second half of the sixteenth century.[8] Even
for Rueda's theater they should not be taken too literally, for the
three men were recording personal memories from thirty to fifty
years after the time of the celebrated goldsmith of Seville. Time
itself as well as unconscious comparison with the popular theaters
(*corrales*) could not help affecting the accuracy of their recollec-
tions.[9]

A second difficulty which confronts the investigator is the ina-
bility to connect a particular dramatic text with a particular kind
of stage. Encina's *Églogas* were performed in a hall (*sala*) of the
Duke of Alba's palace.[10] Diego Sánchez de Badajoz's *Farsa del
Juego de Cañas*[11] and Pedro Suárez de Robles' *Danza del Santíssimo Nacimiento*[12] were played inside a church. Rueda's plays and
many Corpus Christi *autos* like the *Farsa sacramental llamada
Desafío del Honbre*[13] were mounted on platforms (*tablados*) or
floats (*carros*)[14] in the streets and market place. But the performances of most extant plays cannot be determined in this way. For

---

[7] *Don Quixote*, II, 11.
[8] Cf. also, for this view, Cotarelo y Mori, *Obras de Lope de Rueda*, I, xxxv ff.;
E. Walberg, *Juan de la Cueva et son "Exemplar Poetico,"* 110 n.
[9] Cf. Menéndez y Pelayo, "Prólogo" to his edition of *Tres comedias de Alonso
de la Vega*, xiii.
[10] *Teatro completo de Juan del Encina*, ed. Cañete and Barbieri, pp. 3, 75, 89, etc.
[11] See *Recopilación en metro*, II (*Libros de antaño*, XI), Madrid, 1882, pp. 273 SD,
274 SD, 280 SD, 281 SD.
[12] Ed. Gillet, in *PMLA*, XLIII (1928), 614 ff. See 624 SD and Gillet's study,
p. 617.
[13] Performed at Seville in 1570 (Rouanet, *Colección*, IV, 344).
[14] Cf. Sánchez-Arjona, *Anales, passim*.

example, one of the themes most frequently treated by the *autos* was that of the Prodigal Son, but the extant text of the *Aucto del Hijo Pródigo* cannot be definitely associated with any of the known performances.[15] Documentary notices of performances are both rare and brief. Besides, most texts lack an explanatory preface or detailed stage directions which would reveal when, where, and on what sort of stage the plays were presented. It is evident then that an investigation of early staging methods in Spain cannot depend fundamentally on precise knowledge of this kind. Furthermore, it is doubtful whether such knowledge is really as significant as might be supposed. Were plays that were represented in church necessarily staged in a different manner from that applied to performances in the market place or the private palace? The *Representación de los mártires Justo y Pastor*[16] would be a direct refutation of such a theory. This play was performed first on a *carro* in the open air and again a week later in the church of San Justo in Alcalá de Henares. If some details were changed we do not know what they were. The similarity of the two performances must have been very great indeed, for an outdoor *túmulo* was duplicated by another inside the church, and the stage itself (*carro*) was moved inside. It is evident that a method of representation originally intended for one kind of stage could readily be transferred to another.

Other obstacles to the study of early stage practices in Spain are encountered in the general paucity of documentary information on performances and in the lack of iconographical illustrations of stages and dramatic scenes. The scarcity of documentary information is a serious drawback, but nevertheless some significant items are available. They are few in number, brief, and widely scattered. Not only do they need to be collected, but also interpreted in relation to particular plays and particular methods of performance.

The absence of iconography is an equally serious handicap.

[15] Rouanet, *Colección*, IV, 261 ff.
[16] See below, pp. 116-118.

The plastic arts do not portray, to my knowledge, any kind of Spanish stage before the seventeenth century.[17] The manuscripts of Spanish and Catalan plays contain no miniatures of the kind that were so materially helpful in the reconstruction of French medieval stage settings. And title-page woodcuts of old editions are generally unreliable as copies of what really appeared on the stage.[18] Sculpture and paintings may, however, be helpful in one way. Some objects were frequently or regularly represented in art in the same manner. If it is discovered that such an object became a part of the scenery for a play, the stage settings may very well have resembled the conventional form of the object that the spectators were accustomed to seeing in the arts and probably in real life.[19] The value of iconographical evidence should not be exaggerated, however.[20] Even the authoritative French miniatures are valuable only as they corroborate the stage directions and lines of a dramatic text.[21] They complement the text by showing details of costume and setting which might otherwise remain vague, but they do not establish the method of staging. The method for the French *Miracles de Notre Dame* could be, and was, established

[17] The picture of the Corral de la Pacheca, published by Muñoz Morillejo (*Escenografía española*, title page), is apocryphal as the signature of a nineteenth century artist Amalio Fernández [y García] shows.

[18] Woodcuts may be representations of the idea or theme of a work, and not necessarily of a stage production, quite like those that often illustrated non-dramatic works (cf., for example, the title page of López de Yanguas, *Triunphos de Locura*, in Salvá, *Catálogo*, Num. 743). The figurines in Timoneda's *Turiana* prove that woodcuts did not represent costumes worn on the stage. For example, the same block illustrated the king in the *Filomena*, a gentleman named "Facio Andrea padre de Licea" in the *Trapaçera*, and a merchant in the *Rosalina* (*Obras completas de Juan de Timoneda*, edited by M. Menéndez y Pelayo for the Sociedad de bibliófilos valencianos, I, Valencia, 1911, pp. 209, 379, 433). For the long life and changing identity of woodcuts of this kind, cf. Carolina Michaëlis de Vasconcellos, *Autos portugueses de Gil Vicente y de la escuela vicentina*, 60-75; also J. E. Gillet and E. B. Williams, Introduction to their edition of the *Tragedia de los amores de Eneas y de la Reyna Dido*, in *PMLA*, XLVI, 355-356.

[19] The tomb, for example (cf. below, pp. 71-72).

[20] For errors in the conception of English staging methods due to misleading iconography, cf. Lawrence, "Windows in the Pre-Restoration Stage," in *Anglia*, XXXVI (1912), 450 ff.; cf. also Spencer, "How Shakespeare Staged his plays; some notes on the Dubiety of non-textual evidence," in *The Johns Hopkins Alumni Magazine*, XX (1932), 205, 221.

[21] Stuart, "The Stage Setting of Hell and the Iconography of the Middle Ages," in *RR*, IV, 330 ff.

without the aid of miniatures and with the help of only a few stage directions.[22] The early Spanish and Catalan plays present an analogous problem.

In view of the meager stock of information on early stage practices in Spain, the available existing sources must be fully utilized. The chief source which has hitherto been largely neglected is the dramatic texts themselves, more than four hundred of which are now published. The use of a text as a fundamental source depends necessarily on the assumption that the play was performed. This assumption has sometimes been challenged[23] because of the absence of documentary evidence of a performance. But such a challenge is not necessarily final and may be answered by a number of circumstances which strongly favor an assumption of performance.

How is one to explain the existence of several hundred dramatic pieces, if they were not produced before an audience? Dialogued novels like the *Celestina* and its imitations, translations or adaptations like those of Pérez de Oliva, and plays which contain scenic impossibilities like Garnier's in France[24] were doubtless addressed to readers. Moreover such an author as Torres Naharro, whose *Propaladia* went through at least nine editions in half a century, must have had a large reading public.[25] But many plays have been recovered from manuscripts, which could never have reached a large number of readers. Others have been reprinted from rare, unique editions, which hardly prove their literary popularity or wide circulation. Furthermore, the great majority of these texts are of slight literary merit, and it is difficult to imagine the admirers of Garcilaso or even the readers of the chivalric romances taking such great delight in them as their number would suggest. The texts are more understandable as a permanent record of

---

[22] Stuart, *Stage Decoration in France in the Middle Ages*, 54-84. The manuscript miniatures of the French *Miracles* have since been published by Dorothy Penn (see Bibliography).

[23] Mérimée, *L'art dramatique*, 58.

[24] Rigal, *Le théâtre français avant la période classique*, 127.

[25] J. E. Gillet, "Torres Naharro and the Spanish Drama of the Sixteenth Century," in *Estudios eruditos in Memoriam de Adolfo Bonilla y San Martín*, II, 440.

successful performances. Encina's little pieces had been performed over a period of nearly four years before they were included in the Cancionero of 1496. The *argumento* of Juan Pastor's *Farsa de Lucrecia* is preceded by the explanation, "Siguese el argumento, en el qual se declara la hystoria y ponese aqui para los lectores."[26] Had readers constituted the only audience to which Juan Pastor directed his play, there would have been no need of a section written solely for them. The implication is clear that the *argumento* was not necessary for the spectators at a performance, but that the reader, unaided by the acting, costumes, properties and settings of a production, required such a help. This may possibly be the explanation of many prose *argumentos* which introduce plays in verse.

Unless the play was to be performed, how does one account for the dramatist's concern for necessary stage business and settings, expressed in dialogue and stage directions, and for his open appeals to his spectators by addressing them directly in *loas, introitos* and *argumentos?*[27] The dramatist not only had his eye on the stage itself but demonstrates a practical knowledge of his craft born of association with theatrical conditions. Indeed, for all but a few plays, the dramatists' care in avoiding staging impossibilities can readily be demonstrated.

In brief, an explanation of the existence and preservation of many early plays as literary pieces is entirely unconvincing. Besides, the plays usually contain within themselves some indication that they were intended to be performed or were capable of being staged. Of this capacity the only valid test in any given case is whether the play could readily have been performed according to the method and requirements which it imposes upon itself.[28] In the absence of adverse evidence, performance should be assumed

[26] See Bonilla's reprint, in *RHi*, XXVII (1912), 437.
[27] Both Rouanet (*Colección*, I, xi) and Cañete (*Teatro español*, 242) accepted such introductions as proof of performance.
[28] Moratín, in his discussion of Miranda's *Comedia Pródiga*, begs the question entirely when he says the imagination of the spectators compensated for apparent violences and difficulties in staging (*Orígenes*, in *Obras*, I, 191; cf. below, pp. 79-81).

in the case of any play that is free from impossibilities or inconsistencies in the form of staging it requires.

A determination of the method of staging, including the requirements of setting and properties, by means of the dramatic text,
involves one fundamental principle—careful and constant visualization of the play, from beginning to end, as if it were being performed. This procedure is necessary for a contemporary Shaw
or Quintero play with its lengthy directions and with specific knowledge of the kind of stage for which it was intended. It is all the
more necessary for our early plays, the staging of which is unknown to us even in general outlines. All possible systems must
be envisaged, from a bare stage to one completely equipped. Stage
directions which indicate settings either specifically or by implication from the action of the players are of particular value.
Equally important but usually less exact are the lines spoken by
the actors which designate bodily movements or the use of properties and scenery. The process of visualization exacts the greatest
caution in determining the necessary method of performance from
among several possible methods. Care must be exercised in dis-
tinguishing real scenery from imaginary decoration, structural settings or material properties from "spoken" scenery.[29] Only the indispensable minima for the performance of each play should be
insisted upon. To reject scenic elements suggested but not required
by the text may at times involve great injustice to the playwrights
and the stage craftsmen. Indeed many decorative devices may have
been employed which are not even hinted at in the text. But the
basic method of performance cannot be established if the reconstruction depends on any features which may have been possible
but which were not absolutely essential.

The present study is largely based on the method of visualization
just described. The procedure of drawing evidence of staging practices from dramatic texts has frequently been suggested or recommended, either explicitly or by implication, in various studies of

[29] See below, pp. 80 n. 43, 104, 112.

the early drama.[30] Rouanet applied the method repeatedly in matters of costume,[31] Gillet has made some use of it in his studies of three different plays,[32] and the recent study of Williams is based almost exclusively on "internal evidence."[33] My own work represents an attempt to extend systematically a procedure already tried and accepted.

A technique for writing and performing plays developed in Europe during the Middle Ages which required a multiple stage equipped with simultaneous settings. As the liturgical drama grew, the plays and the scenery became more complicated, until the action occurred in two or more places, and the stage decoration representing them was set in its entirety before the action began. This technique included a great imaginative foreshortening of space, when Jerusalem and Nazareth, Paradise and Hell, or any two settings, were separated by only a few feet. Moreover the stage presented great panoramic comprehensiveness and showed a pronounced striving for realistic spectacle. The multiple stage was most elaborately developed in the French *mystères* of the fifteenth and sixteenth centuries, when from five to a dozen settings frequently appeared side by side.[34] The system was followed in simpler form in the Italian *sacre rappresentazioni*,[35] and may also be seen in England in the old Cornish "rounds"[36] and elsewhere.[37] For Spain it

[30] In addition to citations throughout this study, cf., e.g., Sánchez-Arjona, *Anales,* 14; Cotarelo y Mori, *Juan del Encina y los orígenes del teatro español,* 49; Alvarez de la Villa, *Juan del Enzina El Aucto del Repelón,* 315; House, "A Study of Encina and the Egloga Interlocutoria," in *RR,* VII (1916), 459; Mérimée, *L'art dramatique,* 263-264; Crawford, *Spanish Drama,* 71; Schack, II, 259 n. 1 (for seventeenth century).

[31] *Colección,* IV, 172, 283, 295, 335, 336, 340.

[32] See the Christmas plays of Perolópez Ranjel (*PMLA,* XLI [1926], 860 ff.) and Pedro Suárez de Robles (*PMLA,* XLIII [1928], 614 ff.) and the *Tragedia Josephina* of Micael de Carvajal, li-liii.

[33] *The Staging of Plays in the Spanish Peninsula Prior to 1555,* 7. This book reached me just as my monograph was going to press. In it may be found careful analyses of Castilian dramatic texts printed before 1555.

[34] Petit de Julleville, *Histoire du théâtre en France; les mystères;* Cohen, *Histoire de la mise en scène;* Stuart, *op. cit.*

[35] D'Ancona, *Origini,* esp. Book II.

[36] Chambers, *The Mediaeval Stage,* esp. II, 85, 123, 135; cf. also the same author's *The Elizabethan Stage,* esp. III. Sketches of stage plans appear in Norris, *The Ancient Cornish Drama,* I, 219, 479; II, 201. Cf. also *ibid.,* II, 452-457.

[37] Cf. Thorndike, *Shakespeare's Theater,* 6-14.

has been thought scarcely to have existed if we may judge by the persistent silence of critics.[38]

The present study is an examination of the manifestations of the multiple stage technique in Spain from the earliest records of dramatic performances up to the period of Lope de Vega. The multiple stage technique did not cease when Lope began to write plays. Its persistence in the *corrales* as well as in the grouping of *carros* for the *autos sacramentales* has been pointed out.[39] Permanent theaters had been established. A national drama developed in the *comedia* under the leadership of Lope and was presented in these new theaters. At the same time the street and market place saw the flowering of the very special art of the *auto sacramental*. Hundreds of dramatic texts of this period have been preserved to form perhaps the world's most voluminous record of theatrical activity. Documentary evidence is also more abundant than in the earlier years. All these circumstances make the multiple stage in this later period the proper subject of a separate and later study.

The total space of the multiple stage was divided into sections that seemed more like a group of individual stages than parts of a single stage. The sections were mutually independent and yet connected by easy intercommunication. The stage was never a compact unit. In the modern theater a series of scenes involving changes of the place of action involves no change of position on the stage, for the total stage space is treated as a unit. The stage is used as a whole, and it therefore represents one place at a time. Either the imagination or the shifting of scenery changes the identity of the stage. On the multiple stage, however, it is the actors

[38] Mérimée was convinced that the system of staging used for the fifteenth century Valencian Assumption Play was *"celui du décor simultané"* (*L'art dramatique,* 50), and Gillet suggested such a method as possible for the *Tragedia Josephina* in his edition of Carvajal's play (li-liii). Williams, 136, follows Gillet in his characterization of the staging of this play, but he seems to regard it as an isolated example. In a few of his analyses, notably those of Pedraza's *Comedia de Sancta Susaña* (pp. 89-90) and the anonymous *Auto de la quinta angustia* (pp. 92-93), Williams appears to sense the existence of multiple staging. But he invents the term "unlocalized scene" unnecessarily and fails to relate Spanish staging to known European medieval stage practices.

[39] Rennert, *Spanish Stage,* 89 ff.; González Pedroso, *Autos sacramentales,* xli ff.

that shift. They move from one section of the stage to another—
from one place of action to another—bridging miles or infinite distances with a stride.

Because of this treatment of the total space of the stage so characteristic of the multiple system, it is necessary in the interest of
clarity to employ a few terms in a special sense. In this study,
"stage" will mean all the space used by the actors in the representation of a play, and does not necessarily have any reference whatever to a constructed platform or definitely delimited area. "Mansion" applies to any section of the stage that is used to represent
a single place of action and contains scenery or decoration to identi-
fy it steadily as such. "Location" refers to a similar portion of the
stage which depends upon an imaginative acceptance of its identity,
as determined by the distribution and action of the players. In this
study many "locations" may really have been "mansions", but
without evidence of setting, they must remain "locations."

The chief aim of this study is to show the existence and extent
of the multiple stage technique in Spain from its earliest manifestations to the latter part of the sixteenth century. In view of this
primary purpose, matters of staging will be discussed that were
fundamental to the multiple system, such as the use of different
stage levels and the number and kinds of settings employed. Lack
of evidence precludes the general treatment of some aspects of
staging pertinent to the multiple technique. These will, however,
be considered whenever possible in connection with individual
plays. Among them will be included such matters as the place where
the stage was located (church, private house, street, etc.), the arrangement of the settings and locations, and the combination of
the multiple stage method with the modern or consecutive setting
technique.

CHAPTER I

BEFORE THE SIXTEENTH CENTURY

The earliest indications of dramatic performances in Spain yield no information on the methods of representation.[1] It has been conjectured that the twelfth century Castilian *Auto de los Reyes Magos,* of which only a fragmentary text remains, was played in a Toledan church.[2] From the *Siete Partidas* of Alfonso el Sabio it is clear that by the thirteenth century performances were taking place both inside and outside the church, and *juegos de escarnio* were being played in the public square and streets.[3] For the Corpus Christi celebrations of the fourteenth century plays on such religious subjects as the *sacrificio de Isaac* and the *sueño y venta de Jacob* were produced by priests in the open air.[4] But from such meagre information[5] it would be hazardous to attempt any inference as to stage decorations and the technique of performance.

Sufficient records from the fifteenth century remain, however, to indicate that by this time, if not before, the material aspects of staging had definitely become an important consideration. In the Eastern and Northeastern parts of the peninsula pageants and festival performances were equipped with elaborate settings and properties. For the coronation of D. Fernando de Antequera at Zaragoza in 1414, "se construyó un castillo de madera, en cuyo torreón central había un niño, . . . El torreón era el centro de un disco

---

[1] Dramatic or, at least, histrionic activity in Spain goes back to Visigothic and Roman times; its continuity was interrupted by the Moorish invasion and reestablished in the eleventh or twelfth century (see Moratín, *Orígenes,* 58-59; González Pedroso, *Autos sacramentales,* x; Schack, I, 165 ff.).

[2] Baist, *Grundriss,* II, ii, 400; Bonilla, *Las bacantes,* 71.

[3] Partida I, Título VI, Leyes XXXIV and XXXVI. See also Schack, I, 220 and Crawford, "A Note on the Boy Bishop in Spain," in *RR,* XII (1921), 146.

[4] *España sagrada,* XLV, 17. Cf. below, p. 106, for the sixteenth century multiple stage treatment of the sacrifice of Isaac.

[5] Even the existence of a late fourteenth century "tragedy" entitled *L'Hom enamorat y la fembra satisfeta,* which would be the earliest known secular dramatic piece in the peninsula, has now been disproved by Eduardo Juliá in his *estudi crític,* attached to the recent edition of the *Régles de Amor i Parlament de un Hom i una Fembra* obra atribuida al canceller Mossen Domingo Masçó segle XIV [Castelló, 1926], 169-178.

giratorio en el cual iban cuatro doncellas, ... Además en los cuatro ángulos del castillo, había otras tantas torres . . . . "[6] Considerable scenic decoration must have appeared on the two Valencian *entramesos* (*carros* or floats) which represented "paradís e infern" in 1424.[7] And about thirty years later in Barcelona three carts were most elaborately fitted out for the Creation, the Nativity and the Annunciation. The stage for the Bethlehem scene, for example, contained several platforms and pillars, a Heaven and clouds, a manger with the infant Jesus, the ox and the ass, and a door and a stairway.[8] In Castile the Condestable D. Miguel Lucas frequently indulged in entertainment called *entremeses or momos*,[9] which sometimes required scenic decoration. On one occasion a huge dragon's (*serpiente*) mouth was built of wood. At the proper time in the performance it belched forth fiery flames and a host (*infantería*) of young pages came out one by one.[10]

The earliest manifestation of elaborate scenery, however, occurs in connection with the multiple stage technique. At the coronation of D. Martín I in 1399 at Zaragoza, a vertical multiple stage was employed for a religious pageant. Two different levels represented Heaven and Earth, and between them a cloud passed several times,

---

[6] Bonilla, *Las bacantes*, 82. Mérimée says, "ces *entramesos* de Saragosse avaient été prêtés par la ville de Valencia" (*L'art dramatique*, 12 n. 3).

[7] Milá, *Obras*, VI, 246-247.

[8] "Item un altre entramés appellat Bellem alias la Nativitat de Jhus. Xpst. sobre lo buch del qual entramés fará de nou dos porxes ab mitga del hu al altre en cascun dels quals porxes haurá quatra pilars qui tindrán cascun son porxo. E sus cascun dels dits porxos ço es en la sumitat de cascun dels dits pilars haurá un ángel dels quals los quatra tindrán un cel rodó ab nuvols stellat en mig del qual cel se mostrará Deu lo Pare *saltim* de mig amunt quitant raigs de foch ó de lums qui passaran per la difarencia ó spay dels dits dos porxos e bastarán fins baix on sera lo Jesus nat. E baix en lo pla del buch del dit entremés ço es á la part sinistra haurá un presebra en que serán lo bou e l'asa, qui en aquella part stará Josep agenollat. E en laltre porxo de part dreta stará la Maria ajonollada, e en lo mig de la difarencia dels dits dos porxos stará lo infant Jesus tot nuu lensant raigs de si mateix vers lo qual infant los dits Maria e Josep segons dit es stants agenollats contemplarán. E de continent vinguen los III Reys qui munten per la porta del dit entramés, muntant per la scala que aqui fara lo dit mossen Çalom e adorarán l'infant Jesus." (Document of the year 1453 published by Andreu Balaguer, in Milá, *Obras*, VI, 368-371.)

[9] *Cronica del Condestable Miguel Lucas de Iranzo*, in *Memorial histórico español* VIII, 26, 56, 162, 165, 169, 265-266, 312. Moratín called the *momos* which formed a part of the royal entertainment at Soria in 1436 "*acciones cómicas*" (*Orígenes*, 21, 86).

[10] *Op. cit.*, p. 54.

carrying an actor that represented an angel.[11] A similar technique seems to have been used nearly a hundred years later in the same city for the performance of a Christmas play. An expense account of the parish of San Salvador reveals detailed expenditures for "la representacion de la Nativitat de Nuestro Redentor, en la noche de Nadal de 1487." Among the items are amounts paid for materials involved in the making of heavens, stars and clouds.[12] Toward the close of the century, a similarly elaborate setting for Heaven may have become quite customary. For the reception of Isabel la Católica in Barcelona in 1481, a "representacion alegórica de *Santa Eulalia*" was performed, "en la cual había tres cielos girando el uno contra el otro."[13] And for the Corpus Christi festival at Seville in 1497, "para figurar el cielo . . . gastáronse 'dos libras de engrudo para pegar el cielo, 8 libras de algodón para la nube del cielo, cuatro blancas y cuatro azules', 'once papeles de plata dorados para las estrellas e fuegos del cielo', y 'dos cueros [?] para pintar un solio' "; and inside there were a number of people including "ocho 'cantorcillos del coro' con su maestro."[14] A further suggestion of the extensive and popular use of aerial machinery occurs in references to a flying angel in the interpolated shepherd scene in the *Vita Christi* of Frey Iñigo de Mendoça.[15]

[11] ". . . azia la parte de la sala de los mármoles en la techumbre se avia hecho una invencion de grande espectáculo á manera de cielo estrellado que tenia diversas gradas, y en ellas avia diversos bultos de Santos con palmas en las manos, y en lo alto estava pintado Dios Padre en medio de gran muchedumbre de serafines . . . Desde este cielo baxava un bulto grande á manera de nuve, que venia a caer encima del aparador del Rey. De dentro desta nuve baxó uno vestido como ángel cantando maravillosamente; y subiendo y baxando diversas vezes dexávase caer por todas partes muchas letrillas, y coplas escritas, unas en papel colorado, otras . . . etc." (Milá, *Obras*, VI, 236-238.) Four trips in all were made by the Angel to Earth.
[12] ". . . Por media libra de oro de bacin para los cielos y ruedas de los ángeles, 6 s. [ueldos].—Por una piel de oropel para estrellas, 2 s.—Tres libras de aigua cuita para pegar nubes y estrellas, 1 s. 6 d." (Schack, I, 266 n. 1.) Although the clouds may not have been, the *cielos* certainly were practicable, for from earlier items in the account it is certain that the angels were living persons.
[13] See the note of D. José Sol y Padrís to Moratín's *Orígenes*, in *BAE*, II, 153.
[14] Sánchez-Arjona, *Anales*, 5.
[15] Although probably not performed itself, this Encinesque interpolation has often been held to reflect contemporary popular performances (Menéndez y Pelayo, *Antología*, VI, ccx; J. P. W. Crawford, "Pastor and Bobo," in *RR*, II (1911), 380; Bonilla, *Las bacantes*, 89-90; Meredith, *Introito and Loa*, 7). The shepherds see "en el ayre forma humana"; later "llega el angel relumbrando"; and after his departure

The wide use of this kind of two-level stage in Eastern Spain is indicated by the customary representation of the coming of the Holy Spirit, "quod vulgo dicitur la Cometa." In Catalonian territory, throughout the fifteenth and in the first years of the sixteenth century, this popular performance included the mechanical lowering of a dove from Heaven upon the heads of the apostles.[16] In the Cathedral of Valencia this ceremony was accompanied by a grandeur and elaborateness of scenic decoration surpassed by but few other performances. "Construíase un tablado entre el coro y el altar mayor," writes Sanchis y Sivera, "á la altura del presbiterio." On the scaffold were various groups of masked persons representing respectively the apostles, Old Testament characters, pilgrims, "la Virgen . . . en estatua, y las piadosas mujeres. . . . En la parte alta del cimborio hallábanse colocados dos cielos de nubes, uno grande y otro pequeño, formado por diversos lienzos pintados y arreglados de modo especial, donde se veían varios serafines con alas de papel. Las paredes aparecían cubiertas con telas de raso, y se veían, uno enfrente del otro, el sol y la luna, que por un mecanismo especial brillaban y se obscurecían, y según lo exigía el curso de la representación. Pero lo notable, al aparecer, era el mecanismo empleado en lanzar la paloma, que simulaba el Espíritu Santo, desde aquel cielo de telas pintadas que se abría al estruendo de bombardas y otras armas, las que no deberían ser pocas, dada la cantidad de pólvora que se gastaba. Al funcionar *les poliches per tancar y obrir lo cel,* y por una combinación de ruedas arriba y abajo, salía velozmente la *palometa* empujada *per lo moviment de un molinet,* echando fuego en todas direcciones, producido por varios cohetes en ella colocados, y al mismo tiempo bajaban *cresoletes* encendidas, simulando lenguas de fuego, por medio de

one shepherd remarks to another, "el hombre que bolaua, oyste como cantaua" (*Cancionero castellano del siglo XV,* pub. by R. Foulché-Delbosc, I [*NBAE*, XIX], Madrid, 1912, p. 18, col. 2, line 5; 19-3-3; 20-1-8 and 9).
    [16] Villanueva, *Viaje literario,* XVI, 90-92; "Usóse esto en todo el siglo XV, en que solían pagarse ochenta sueldos al que dirigía la máquina. También consta el gasto de almuerzo y merienda á los que representaban los apóstoles, sobre quienes bajaba la paloma." For a general treatment of this device in the Latin plays of the Middle Ages, see Young, *The Drama of the Medieval Church,* I, 489-491.

una combinación de ruedas *damunt e davall,* movidas por el funcionamiento de otras ruedas mayores colocadas no sabemos dónde.[17]

Documentary evidence indicates that in pantomimic performances of the fifteenth century the horizontal multiple stage was also used. At least two locations appeared on one level in the Epiphany play which was performed at Jaen in 1462 in the palace of the Condestable de Castilla D. Miguel Lucas. The chronicler has left a detailed description of the performance: " . . . entró por la sala una dueña cavallera en un asnito sardesco, con un niño en los brazos, que representaba ser nuestra Señora la Virgen María con el su bendito y glorioso fijo, y con ella Joseph." The "condestable la recibió y la subió arriba á el *asiento* do estaba . . . y el dicho señor se retrajo á una camara que está *á el otro cabo de la sala.* Y dende á poco, salió de la dicha camara con los pages mui bien vestidos, con visajes y sus coronas en las cabezas, á la manera de los tres Reyes Magos, y sendas copas en las manos con sus presentes. Y asimismo vino por la sala adelante mui mucho paso y con mui jentil contenencia, *mirando el estrella que los guiaba, la qual iva por un cordel que en la dicha sala estaba, y asi llegó al cabo de ella do la Virgen con su fijo estaba,* y ofreció sus presentes . . . . "[18]

This performance required very little scenery, and apparently the stage did not contain simultaneous settings. At one point however and for several moments thereafter, the stage must have suddenly expanded and subdivided in the imagination. When the Condestable and the pages reentered the room as the Magi, the spectators were confronted with a stage stretching the entire length or width of the hall. At one end the Virgin was seated with the child as if in the stable at Bethlehem, and at the other the Three Kings were beginning their search for the new-born king. The imaginary distance between the two sides of the room was very great. The kings could not see the object of their search at the other

---

[17] Sanchis y Sivera, *La dramática en nuestra catedral,* 6-7. The description quoted here represents an interpretation and synthesis of items in the *Libre de obres* for the year 1463.

[18] *Mem. hist. esp.,* VIII, 75-76.

side of the room and could arrive there only by following the star. The stage was reduced to a single location again only when the Magi reached Bethlehem.[19]

Fortunately we are not entirely confined to such fragmentary information for our knowledge of the *mise en scène* prior to the sixteenth century. Eight dramatic texts have survived which reveal in a more complete manner both the nature and the use of the scenery and properties of the stage. Three of the texts are Valencian mysteries, the performances of which were intended for the Corpus Christi festival and which were eventually represented on *rocas*.[20] Two others are Majorcan *consuetas* (sacred plays) of early but uncertain date.[21] And three are Assumption plays performed inside the church on August 14th and 15th: one Catalonian, another Valencian, and the third from the Levantine town of Elche. Of these plays, all but one, the Valencian *Misteri de San Christofol*,[22] undoubtedly required a multiple stage for their performance.

The multiple stage for the *Misteri de Adam y Eva*[23] contained

[19] This dramatic episode had been performed in 1460 (*ibid.*, 42-43) and was probably an annual affair ("Esta fiesta fazia y solemnizaba el dicho señor Condestable cada un año."—p. 76; cf. also pp. 108, 160).

[20] Serrano Cañete, *El Misterio de Adam y Eva*, 5; Alcahalí, *La música en Valencia*, 96 ff.; Mérimée, *L'art dramatique*, 11. The earliest recorded use of the *entramés* or *roca*, as equivalent to the Castilian *carro*, is of the year 1402.

[21] One of these, the *Consueta del Juy*, is reserved for later discussion (see below, Chap. II, pp. 40-41, 51-52, 59), since in its present form it may belong to the sixteenth century.

[22] The text was printed by Alcahalí, in *La música en Valencia*, 100-105, and edited by Corbató, *Los Misterios del Corpus de Valencia*, 93-98 (94 lines). Textual references will be to the latter. The extant text is scarcely explicit enough to necessitate a multiple stage. Although its first known appearance on a *roca* was in 1587, the play has been known to exist perhaps since 1449. As the extant text dates from the latter part of the fifteenth century, the church may have first served as its stage and theater (Corbató, 61, 69, 85). The only clue for the staging occurs in a stage direction which reads: "Ara pasen tots junts una u dos uegades . . . [fins que] . . . los ague pasat que torna a son lloch (70; see Mérimée, *L'art dramatique*, 25, for a complete analysis of the plot; cf. also Milá, *Obras*, VI, 225-226; Corbató, 43-46). The performance may have utilized a body of water, through which the giant saint waded as he transported his passengers from one side of the river to the other. Although the water may conceivably have been imaginary, the use of actual water on the stage would not be without a parallel (see below, p. 112 n. 146). This text is, however, merely a fragment of a larger work (Corbató, 27). It would be dangerous to conjecture what the stage for the performance of the whole must have been.

[23] The text published by Serrano Cañete is a Castilian translation of the Valencian text. The latter is printed in Alcahalí, 109-120, and Corbató, 99-112 (278 ll.). See

different levels for Heaven and Earth. On the Earth level appeared a setting for the Garden of Eden and perhaps another location for the "world" also.[24] The play opens as follows: "Comensa lo Deu y ans de comensar se obri lo sel ab molta musica mentres que baxa hi en ser en terra, . . ." (1 SD). After creating Adam and Eve and turning Paradise over to them, "lo Deu . . . sen puja al sel" (32 SD). Then Adam and Eve "se alsen y uan pasejant lo paradis" (32 SD). After Adam has lain down to sleep, Eve continues wandering alone "per lo paradis contemplant les plantes y flors" (56 SD). Meanwhile a bit of pantomine has been enacted by the serpent, for in the midst of one of Eve's speeches, a stage direction reads: "Ara sen puja la serpent al abre" (52 SD). After the serpent's successful persuasion, "Pren Eua la mansana y la mosega" (107 SD). Adam's resistance is finally broken down (123-215 SD), and immediately God's voice orders the angel to drive them out of Paradise. The order is obeyed and "Adam y Eua uan iunts" (253 SD), finally receiving, however, the angel's promise of the future redemption.

It is evident that Heaven was constructed at some distance above the stage and that it served as a location for God. A machine brought God to Earth and took Him up to Heaven again—very likely such a form of *araceli* (or *aracoeli*) as was used in the Assumption plays.[25] The Garden of Eden contained a tree, to which the apple may have been attached, and very likely some additional floral and arboreal decoration.[26] The Earth level may possibly have included a second location for the world outside Paradise. Al-

---

Mérimée, *L'art dramatique*, 27-28 for a careful analysis of the play. Cf. also Milá, *Obras*, VI, 222-225. The first recorded appearance of this play on a *roca* was in 1517 (Corbató, 71).

[24] The manuscript seems to have been "destinado al director de la compañia de representantes (Serrano Cañete, 4) and yields interesting information on the costumes of the actors as well as on the stagecraft of the performance.

[25] See below, pp. 27 ff. That such a machine became customary in this performance is proved in a later document published by Corbató, where instructions are given for the building of Heaven and God's throne (pp. 76, 154).

[26] In 1517 five *sous* were paid "per cipres, canyes, e altra rama, e per treball de enramar dita roqua" (Corbató, 71, 150). In the manuscript itself, where the stage decoration is never indicated or described for its own sake, the tree is accorded incidental mention in connection with "lo uestit de la serpent que esta en un rabo penchant als sarguells" (*ibid.*, 92).

though no setting for it is indicated, and no material barrier between Eden and the world seems to have been present,[27] Adam and
Eve were definitely outside Paradise during the last twenty-five
lines of the play.[28] For the *Misteri de Adam y Eva* the vertical
multiple stage was a necessity and the horizontal at least a possibility.

The multiple stage on one level was clearly used for the *Misteri
del Rey Herodes*,[29] a play which belongs to the same stage of theatrical development as the Adam and Eve mystery, although the
date of its present form is quite uncertain.[30] Accompanied by a
page, Melchior, King of Tarsis, sets out in search of the Messiah
(1-62). They follow the star, presently meet Gaspar and Baltasar,
and all continue the journey to Jerusalem (63-110). They seem
to leave the stage ("Entrem," 123), and the place of action suddenly shifts to a council chamber where Herod is questioning two
Sabis about the Messiah. After being announced by *Alguasil,* the
three pages of the Magi appear before Herod (175-178), as do
the Magi themselves a little later (198 ff.). Herod orders them to
find the Messiah and to return to him with the news. The departure of the three kings is indicated as follows:

> "Herodes Señors, vagen en bon ora.
> Y entrem, que ha molt que stich fora,
> ques cas de gran estrañesa.
> Gaspar Est es cami de Belem
> Baltasar ¿ No ueu ¿ia es exit lo estel"   (291-295)

[27] Mérimée's words, "L'ange pousse les coupables vers la porte du paradis," can
only imply an imaginary door or an exit (*L'art dramatique,* 28).
[28] For the Corpus Christi celebrations of 1538 in Mexico City, Indian natives
performed in their own language a play on Adam and Eve which, in many respects,
resembles the earlier Valencian work. The play was mounted according to the multiple
stage technique, two different settings being used for the earth level, one for Paradise
and the other for *Mundo, where a long scene is developed after the expulsion.* Paradise
in particular was decorated with a profusion of animals and birds (real and imaginary),
plants and flowers, mountains and rocks, two trees, and a *puerta* guarded by an
angel (Fernán González de Eslava, *Coloquios espirituales y sacramentales,* pub. by
Joaquín García Icazbalceta, México, 1877, xiii-xvi).
[29] Corbató, 113-114 (593 ll.).
[30] *Ibid.,* 23, 27 and n. 18, 87, 72; Mérimée, *L'art dramatique,* 36. The earliest
documentary evidence associates it with the Corpus celebration of 1571, and the
only descriptions of its performance belong to a period much later than the sixteenth
century (Corbató, 72, 84-85 and nn.). The action of the play is longer and more
complicated than that of the other Valencian mysteries. Although it may occasionally
have been divided into three parts, the Herod mystery was originally a dramatic
unit (Milá, *Obras,* VI, 226-227; Corbató, 56, 73).

Evidently Herod and his advisers leave the stage, the place of action changes to the road once more, and the Magi recommence their journey. They soon reach Bethlehem (298-299), and Melchior exclaims to his page,

> "Mirau en aquex portal,
> ho en exa pobre establia
> deu ser nat lo verp Mesies." (302-304)

Page calls, "¡A de casa! ¿ay algu? (306), to which Joseph immediately answers, "¿Qui es? ¿que manen, señors?" (307). Mary shows the infant Jesus to the three Kings, who then present their gifts (310-348).

A "Memoria de la Roba que se acostuma a donar en la casa de les roques pera els Autos," which appears in the same manuscript as the text, mentions "lo portalet, la estela, la rella" (doorway, star, grating). The doorway and the grating evidently constituted the setting for Bethlehem, and were apparently in sight throughout the play.[31] But the scene of action was often imagined at a great distance from the *portalet*. Therefore at least one other location was necessary for the successive representation of the other places of action—Tarsis, the roadway and the meeting place of the Kings, Jerusalem, Herod's council chamber, and the roadway again.

Another circumstance later in the play further demonstrates the dual location technique. Three reapers are discussing their work, when suddenly one of them exclaims, "Gent es que ue de cami" (388). A twenty-line dialogue between Joseph and Mary immediately follows. They are travelling along the road toward Egypt. Finally Joseph remarks, "Uns llauradors ueig alla" (405), and a few lines later, greetings are exchanged. At the beginning of this scene the Holy Family and the reapers must have been stationed at different locations. One group moves toward the other, and the two groups become united on one location only when salutations are exchanged.

A similar situation occurs a little later. The reapers have begun to harvest the grain, when suddenly the dialogue shifts to *Caualler*

---

[31] If the *portalet* were represented as a backstage, hidden from the spectators until used in the action, it is difficult to see the function of the grating. Cf. also below, pp. 97 ff.

and *Alguasil,* who are traveling along the road in pursuit of the fugitives (431 ff.). Their approach to the reapers is similar to the earlier movement of the Holy Family from one part of the stage to another. Here the imaginary division of the stage into two distinct locations is even more marked. As they travel along, Caualler and Alguasil converse for twelve lines, before they see the reapers at the other location (443). Since in this scene neither location can be the *portalet* of Bethlehem, at this point in the play the stage contained at least two locations in addition to the Bethlehem setting.

The *Misteri del Rey Herodes* was obviously capable of being mounted on a multiple stage of almost any extension. A mansion for Herod and scenery or properties for the wheat field may have been provided. Indeed each location may have had its decoration. The simplest possible staging, however, would have included the doorway as setting for Bethlehem and two or more undecorated locations for all the other places of action.[32]

If the *rocas* in this early period did not lend themselves to any very elaborate or complicated use of the multiple stage technique, quite the reverse was true of the churches themselves.[33] Inside their walls took place performances of the three extant Assumption plays and of a Majorcan play on the temptation of Christ.[34] The oldest is the Catalonian *Assumpció de madona Sta. María,* which dates from the early fifteenth century.[35] The dialogue, partly sung

[32] Herod's location may have been furnished with a chair or bench, as was customary in the sixteenth century (cf. below, pp. 69 n. 19, 74 n. 28, 101). The function of the star during the first part of the play may indeed have been that of moving from location to location, by means of some arrangement similar to that in the Jaen Christmas play (cf. above, p. 15) or to that frequently employed in non-Spanish manifestations of the *Officium Stellae,* as, e.g., in the eleventh century Latin play at Limoges (Du Méril, *Les origines latines du théâtre moderne,* 153: ". . . stellam pendentem in filo, quae antecedit eos, . . .").

[33] Cf. Mérimée, *L'art dramatique,* 56.

[34] Only for the Catalonian *Asumpció,* is specific information lacking as to the place of its performance (cf. Pedrell, 39 n. 2).

[35] The text was published with two other short pieces by Joan Pie under the misleading title "Autos sagramentals del sigle XIV," in *Revista de la Asociación artístico-arqueológica Barcelonesa,* 1893 (Año 2º), 673-686 (Julio-agosto, num. 9), 726-744 (Septiembre-octubre, num. 10).

In a very brief introduction to the texts, the editor stated that the play dates from the fourteenth century, adducing as proof a letter which is signed by "berenguer claris batle de prades" (p. 674), which terminates with the words "Scrita en prades

and partly spoken, is preceded by a long and detailed direction for the arrangement of the stage and interspersed with frequent long and specific directions which leave no doubt about the use of the multiple stage technique. The manuscript begins as follows: "En lo loch hon se fará aquesta representació sia ordenat ayxi com se segueix. Primerament quels juheus facen una bella barracha hont estiguen. Itm lucifer ab los altres diables facen un loch quey sía infern gran. E duguenhi anclusa e mayls per ço que facen gran brogit can hora sirá. Itm sía ordonat parays ab beles porpres e ab richs draps é benes ó clos hon estiga Jesus ab angels é ab archangels. E sent Johan babtista e patriarches é profetes é vergens e daltres mols sans. Itm sía feyta una casa hon estiga Sta. María en la qual aga un bell lit tot encortinat de beles cortines e davant la casa haga un bell horatori hon la verge faça sa oració. Itm sía feyt *En altre loch* un bell sepulcre hon metran la verge María can exirá d'esta vida e aqui aga unes belles vestidures blanques que vista santa María can Jesus la resucitará. E la sen menará a Parays." (p. 674).

It is evident that the play was to be performed on a stage which contained at least five mansions: the cabin of the Jews, Hell, Paradise, the Virgin's house, and the tomb. A stage direction then orders the movement of the angel from Mary's house to Paradise and indicates some noise-making equipment for the Paradise setting.[36] Just before the play begins all the actors "sien justats En un loch é facen lurs intrades" (p. 675). The four groups of players enter in order, each going to its respective setting. Hell's angels lead the procession and are followed first by the Jews, second by the angels, patriarchs and prophets, each with some characteristic

---

a X de marçh lany 1420" (p. 674), and which is written in the same hand as the text of the play. Rouanet (*RHi*, VIII [1901], 541); Mérimée (*L'art dramatique*, 51); and Bonilla (*Las bacantes*, 80) accept and repeat D. Joan Pie's dating. Yet not a single reason has been suggested for placing the date of the play earlier than the recorded date of the letter. The play may be very much older than the letter, but its present manuscript form, by which alone we know it, cannot antedate by very much the identical handwriting marked with the year 1420.

[36] "Itm sia ordonat que quan langel aura duyta la palma á la verge maría can sen tornará á parays que sia feyt brogit ab esclafidos e cerredos En ves parais" (pp. 674-675).

attribute,[37] and finally by the Virgin Mary, who is accompanied by attendants "as far as her house."[38]

After the players are all stationed, each in his proper mansion, the action begins with a general milling of Jews about the stage.[39] Presently they are summoned to the *barracha*, which is "en manera de casa de conseyl."[40] There the Jews make various suggestions for the cremation of the Virgin Mary. The scene then shifts from the *barracha* to the house of Our Lady, who comes out to her chapel to pray.[41] When she has finished praying, the spectators' attention is directed to Paradise, where Jesus orders an angel to carry a palm to his mother. After her acceptance, "Tornsen langel en parais e sia feyt brogit. E sent Johan vingua a la porta de sta. María . . . " (p. 679), as the apostles do later (p. 680 SD). Just before Mary's death St. John steps out of the Virgin's house to explain her imminent death to the apostles. The latter then enter the house and place Our Lady upon the bed.[42]

The scene now shifts to Hell. Astarot, Barit, and Beemot in turn refuse to carry out Lucifer's order to act against the Virgin, and they receive a beating for their disobedience. The punishment of Astarot is indicated as follows: "Aprés los diables *meten starot en infern* e façen molt brogit quax quil bat."[43] It is evident first that the devils stepped out of Hell at the beginning of their scene and Lucifer's orders were given outside, else "meten starot en infern" would be unexplainable, and second that the tortures of Hell were not seen nor realistically represented by visible properties, but only suggested by sound. Indeed, the devils were in this very position

[37] P. 675—". . . porten devant en lurs mans ço que ja han *acostumat de portar.*"
[38] P. 675—"entro á la casa."
[39] P. 675—"trafeguen per lo loch hon se fará la representació."
[40] P. 675;—"vinguen tots á la casa del conseyl . . ." (p. 676); not inappropriately does Bonilla refer to the structure as their *aljama* (*Las bacantes,* 79).
[41] "Itm. can los juheus auran dit ço que adirán la verge María exirá de la sua casa e devotament ahorará en son horatori" (p. 675).
[42] "Aprés isqua sent johan de la casa de sta. María . . . Pux entren los apostols e homilment enclínense á la verge María . . . De pux posen sta. María en lo lit e sien encees molts ciris que tinguen los apostols hordonat apres lo lit e sent pere e sent pau al cap del lit e los altres apres" (p. 682 SD's).
[43] P. 683. Similar treatment of Barit is directed thus: "E los diables façen axí com del primer" (p. 684).

when Mascarón[44] complied with Lucifer's command, the stage
direction reading: "Puys *estiguen fora dinfern* los diables e masca-
ron pus prop de la casa de Sta. María . . . " (p. 685).
After being
beaten back by Jesus with the cross, all return to hide in Hell,[45]
never again to appear in the play.
A group of saints, leaving their fellows in Paradise, now accom-
pany Jesus to Mary's house where they gather about the bed.
Christ takes the Virgin's soul and then returns to Paradise in the
company of the saints.[46]
The attention of the spectators is now drawn away from Heaven
and back to the Virgin's house where the apostles are making
preparations for the burial. But at the same time one eye is drawn
to the mansion of the Jews, who are pretending to sleep.[47] After
some discussion, "leuen lo lit los apostols" (p. 728 SD), and "Com
los apostols *siran davant* los juheus façen apares los juheus ques
desperten prenent les armes" (p. 729 SD). At the first movement of
attack, the Rabí is held as if fastened to the bed and unable to free
himself, and all the others become blind. The Rabí must accept
God, Jesus and Mary without reservation and kiss the funeral bed
of the Virgin. Only then are the Jews released from the miraculous
plague temporarily placed upon them.[48] They soon "tornensen a la

[44] The suggestion for this part of the play may indeed have been taken from
the Processus Belial. The early Catalan narrative entitled *Mascarón* (pub. by Bofarull
y Mascaró, in *Colección de documentos inéditos del archivo general de la corona
de Aragón*, XIII, 107-117) may have been recited as a monologue (Milá, VI, 216).
Cf. also Alenda, *BRAE*, V (1918), 673; Bofarull, *op. cit.*, 6; *BAE*, II, 152 n; Crawford, "The Catalan *Mascarón* and an episode in Jacob van Maerlant's Merlijn," in
PMLA, XXVI, (1911), 47. In the Assumption play Mascarón is still Lucifer's agent,
but the rôle is quite subordinate and he could scarcely now be called the devil's
advocate.
[45] "Puys los diables amaguense en infern fen gran brugit" (p. 685).
[46] "Puys vingua Jesuchrist ab alguna companya dels sants els altres romanguen
en parays . . ." (p. 685). ". . . Com será Jesús davant sta. María facen loch los
apostols e hordense Jesus ab los altres sans en torn del lit . . ." (p. 686). ". . .
Lavos prengua Jesus la anima de Sta. María . . . Lavos Jesuchrist ab tota sa
companya tornsen aparais . . ." (pp. 726-727).
[47] "Pux los juheus façen apares que dormen e estiguen tots ab ses armes e
los apostols apparelense de portar lo cors . . ." (p. 727 SD).
[48] "E pux lo Rabí exech se en ves lo lit quax quil vol enderoquar e estigua
penjat per lo lit a manera com qui no sen pot deslapaçar e tots los altres juheus
façen apares que sien orbs e que no sapien anar . . ." (p. 729 SD). "Dit aço
yequescas caure del lit e yagua en terra doloreyanse . . ." (p. 730 SD).

barrcha e puys los apostols . . . prenguen lo lit . . . e porten lo cors ala soboltura" (p. 731 SD). Christ joins the group at the tomb, and after some ceremony the soul of the Virgin is carried to Paradise and crowned.[49] And thus, after some singing, is ended the *Asumpció de madona Sta. María.*

Even if the extant manuscript did not include such a careful preliminary account of the setting, the necessity for the simultaneous presence of the five decorated locations will now be evident from the action of the play. Hell was used simultaneously with the Virgin's house and Paradise, for as Mascarón, proceeding from Hell, reached the house, he was met by Jesus, who had just come from Paradise. Again, when Jesus had driven all the devils back into Hell and was on the point of returning, he was joined by a group of saints from Paradise who then accompanied him to the Virgin's house. Later four of the settings were involved in a continuous series of actions. The funeral procession commenced at the Virgin's house and, on its way to the tomb, was interrupted by the attack of the Jews. When this had been effectively repulsed, the group continued on its way to the sepulchre.[50] Jesus had meanwhile left Paradise and made his way also to the burial location, where he joined the apostles.

The least used mansion was Hell. Within it a great deal of noise was made, but we have scarcely any notion of its appearance. It was large and was built on the stage. There is no suggestion that it was placed on a lower level. The interior of Hell was probably not seen by the spectators for it was used by the devils as a place of concealment ("amaguanse"). In later dramatizations of the Assumption theme Hell disappeared altogether. Indeed it played an insignificant part in all the known old Spanish theaters. We might

---

[49] "Apres amaguan la anima trguenla [*sic*] del sepulcre e portla en paradis cantant . . ." (p. 732 SD), "Com sien en parais pos la Jesus a la dreta part e posli la corona el cap . . ." (p. 733 SD). The soul of the Virgin actually sings to the people just before the end (p. 725). When it was taken to Heaven the first time it may possibly have been represented by a doll (cf. below, p. 70 n. 20).

[50] Bonilla was obviously quite wrong in placing the meeting of apostles and Jews before the tomb (*Las bacantes,* 80), since the stage direction indicates a further march to the burial spot.

say that this popular medieval French *maison* met with slight favor south of the Pyrenees from its earliest adoption.[51]

The *barracha* of the Jews was beautiful and looked like a *casa de conseyl*. The tomb was also beautiful, and large enough to permit the actor to put on his white robes without being seen by the audience. Whether a sub-stage level was available for this operation is not stated. If it was, we may reasonably imagine a tomb of the low flat stone variety, almost the only type found in the iconography of the period.[52]

The mansion for Heaven was evidently placed on the same stage level as the others. The absence of any suggestion that it was raised above the level of the other settings may be considered equivalent to disproof of an uppel level.[53] Such a conclusion is particularly justifiable for this play, since its text is otherwise so replete with minute details regarding the action of the players and their relation to the setting. Heaven must have been quite large to accommodate such a considerable group of saints and prophets as seems to have gone there at the opening of the play. Its only decoration may have been the beautiful draperies and a few chairs.

The setting for the Virgin was doubtless the most elaborate of all. Furnished with a bed which was itself curtained off from the rest of the mansion, it seems to have resembled an actual house or room. It possessed a real door, and the Virgin's movement to the adjacent or connected chapel is treated as an exit from the house.

The arrangement and relative positions of the five settings cannot be determined definitely. It would seem, from the necessities involved in the episode of the Jews, that the *barracha* lay between the Virgin's mansion and the tomb. Hell may have been at one end of the stage and Paradise at the other, as was the regular French

[51] Cf. below, pp. 48 ff. (II). For the possible influence of French mystery plays on the early theater in the peninsula, see Corbató, 33 ff., and Pons, *La littérature catalane en Rousillon au XVII⁰ et au XVIII⁰ siècle*, 237.

[52] Cf. below, p. 72.

[53] There is no foundation for Bonilla's statement that "el alma de la Virgen asciende al Paraíso" (*Las bacantes*, 80).

custom.[54] It may be suggested, then, that the settings were placed in a row or a semi-circle in the following order: Paradise, tomb, *barracha*, Virgin's house, and Hell.

A Majorcan play entitled *Consueta de la representacio de la tentatio que fonch feta a nro. se. xpt.*[55] preserves another record of simultaneous staging in the Catalonian drama. Although less elaborate the *Consueta* required a method of staging not unlike that of the *Assumpció*.

While St. John and a publican are conversing in the opening scene, ". . . es menester que Jesus vinga per la sglesia [sic] amunt devers alla on ses fet lo batisme . . . " (p. 128, col. 1 SD). He pauses there to recite a few verses, and then passes on to join St. John and his companion (p. 128-2 SD). A stage direction then reads: "Es menester que Deu lo Pare stiga a un cadefal ab sos Angels los que el voldrá y trameta vna coloma feta ab vn artifici que vinga sobre lo cap de Jesus com se ferá lo baptisme . . ." (p. 128-2 SD), and a few lines later "Are sen tornará la coloma de Deu lo Pare y lo Iesus an el desert a fer oració" (p. 129-1 SD). While Jesus is shifting from one place to another and during St. John's eight-line speech, "Es menester que sian aplegats set dimonis y tingan consell del modo que se a de temptar lo Jhūs . . . y Lucifer . . . sta asegut en my dells, ab vna gran cora y vna corona en lo cap, a son cadefal . . . (p. 129 SD's). After each of the devils has recommended a way to tempt our Lord, "Are canta lo Jesus en el desert . . . (p. 131-2 SD) and "Are com lo Ihs. cantará, Bersabuch lo aguaytará y anirá a Lucifer" (p. 131-2 SD). The devils then dress Lucifer in the garb of a hermit "y anirá deues lo desert, hon es lo Jesus" (p. 133-1 SD). During their debate "sen van [Lucifer y Jesus] a un loch alt" (p. 133-1 SD), later "Are van a un loch mes alt . . . (p. 133-2 SD), and finally ". . . . Lucifer lansará las robes de ermita y fugirá y tots

los altres lo alepideran. Dirá Deu lo pare . . . tremetra los angels
a nel Jesus . . . " (p. 133-2 SD). The angels go to Jesus (p. 134-
1 SD), and the play concludes with a "Te deum".
This text contains no preliminary directions for the arrangement of the stage, as did Joan Pie's manuscript. Nevertheless,
from the stage directions and dialogue alone, it is evident that at
least four locations were required for a performance inside a
church. Two were platforms for God and his angels and for
Lucifer. A third was the desert, which seems to have contained
some structure with two elevations for the successive heights to
which Jesus and Lucifer climbed. The fourth was the space adjacent to and probably including the baptismal font. This location
may perhaps have encompassed the place where the conversation
between St. John and the publican took place at the beginning of
the play. If not, a fifth location is indicated for the opening scene.
The first three locations were equipped with settings—mansions
for Heaven, Hell and the mountain. The use of the dove seems
to resemble the ceremony of the *Colometa*. If it was transported
from God to Jesus by means of the *araceli*, the platform for God
may have been quite high. Both the elevations and the platforms
were more characteristic of the Valencian than of the early Catalonian *mise en scène*. The platform for Lucifer may however have
been very slightly raised above the ground. Furthermore the
upper level was still like the French *Paradis*—a platform connected materially with the Earth and rising from it.

A two-day Valencian Assumption play[56] was almost contempo-
raneous with the Catalonian *Asumpció* but differed markedly from

[56] The fifteenth century manuscript was published by Alcahalí, 83-91. Mérimée
has discussed the play in detail and has given it the title, *Assomption et Mort de la
Vierge* (*L'art dramatique*, 45-46). The text appears to be an actor's copy for the
part of the Virgin and belongs linguistically to the first years of the century.
Alcahalí offers as one reason for his dating the piece prior to the Catalonian *Asumpció*,
or, as he thought, in the fourteenth century, the fact that the *judiada* does not appear
in the Valencian play, arguing that its absence marks the work as simpler and
therefore earlier than the Catalonian play, which does contain the attack of the
Jews. If such an argument were in itself conclusive we should have to move forward
about two centuries the date of the sixteenth century Castilian *auto* which lacks this
episode (Rouanet, *Colección*, III, Num. LXII; cf. below, pp. 81-83).

it in settings and method of staging. Performed inside the church,[57] it employed at times a cast of characters that must have rivalled in magnitude that of Max Reinhardt's colossal modern production, the *Miracle*.[58] The Virgin's house is again the most elaborate mansion, and the tomb may have been similar to the Catalonian setting. But Hell and the Jew's cabin are entirely absent, and the setting for Heaven has undergone a radical transformation. Furthermore, the *araceli* accomplishes, by descent and ascent, those miraculous connections between Heaven and Earth. And three or four additional settings, "lieux qui ont vu l'agonie de son fils,"[59] are used for a pilgrimage made by the Virgin just after the play begins.

The setting for the Virgin is a "cambra" located on a scaffold, constructed to include a real entrance door equipped with a knocker, and furnished with a chair and a bed.[60] At the outset of the play, Mary determines to make the pilgrimage, "leuse de son setial euaiasen onestamēt entorn la cambra tro ala porta e hixquasen e uaia uisitar los santuaris . . ." (p. 84). Her changes of position from one setting to another are proved by such stage directions as: "E quant la maria sera dauāt lort de cherico agenol se . . . ," "leuse dempes e deuotamēt faça huna humiliacio del cap e uaiassen amonticaluari. E quan sera dauant la creu agenolse . . . ," "e apres la maria uaga sen al sepulcre e agenolse . . . ," "E acabada la cobla uaia abesar lo sepulcre e uaia sen amōt olivet . . . ," "E puys tornesen deuotament ala casa e quant sera ala porta gir se deuers lo altar e puys entre sen e sigas en son sitial" (pp.

---

[57] Two stage directions specifically consider the interests of the audience: (1) "per tal que lo poble vega la maria" (p. 84); (2) "per ço que tot hom la uega" (p. 90). Two others refer definitely to the altar and the choir: (1) "quant sera [Maria] ala porta girse deuers lo altar" (p. 85); (2) "E aixi uagen tro adauāt ala porta del cor e aqui la maria faca estacio estant girada uers laltar" (p. 90).

[58] A series of stage directions brings into a procession before the Virgin "los apostols," "gamaniel e lazer ab los altres," "lo poble," "les maries," "les donzelles dela maria," "dones e donzelles" (p. 90).

[59] Mérimée, *L'art dramatique*, 46.

[60] "Quant la maria sa en lo quadafal mūtada uaiasen ala cambra sua . . . e entresen per la porta ab ses dues donzelles . . . E quant sera al setial asigras onestament" (p. 84). ". . . los apostols e p̄nceps e altres munten la maria sobre lo lit" (p. 88). For St. John's arrival at the Virgin's house, the stage direction reads ". . . uinga lo iohan ala porta dla maria e toque alanella . . ." (p. 86 last line).

84-85). The simultaneous setting of these places—all of them probably on the scaffold, as Mérimée assumes[61]—is beyond doubt, although the cross and the tomb are the only scenic elements definitely indicated. On the second day the *sepulcre* for the Virgin was also stationed on the platform. From a compartment below smoke and a noise as of thunder would frequently issue. This compartment also served as the hiding place where the living Virgin and the image could be interchanged.[62] Before the ascent to Heaven the Virgin was removed from the tomb and returned to her house in front of the choir and opposite the high altar.[63]

Heaven was a practicable structure which could open and close, located under the dome of the church.[64] It was not a platform or scaffold rising from the Earth level, but rather like a sky suspended from above. The *araceli* provided the means for the actors' descent. It lowered its occupants (Angel, Jesus) from the dome-Heaven to the platform below, directly in front of the Virgin's setting.[65] The *Araceli* also carried images representing Jesus and Our Lady's spirit back to Heaven.[66]

[61] "Sur cette estrade on simulait un décor multiple" (*L'art dramatique,* 49). If the action of the play moved off the scaffold, we would expect to find some indication of it in the text, which in other matters presents such careful and complete directions.
[62] P. 89—"los quj son dauall lo cadafal . . . faent grans trons e pfums e hixqua soptosament la uiua." P. 91—"facen trons efums e entresen secretamēt lo IHS e la maria." P. 89—"e meten la maria dauall lo cadafal. Etraguen la ymage e facen tot laltre offiici" (p. 89).
[63] P. 90—"traguen la maria del moniment . . . E aixi uagen tro adauāt ala porta del cor e aqui la maria faca estacio estant girada uers laltar."
[64] Stage directions read as follows: (1) "obras lo cel" (p. 88); (2) "los angels del cembori canten" (p. 91). If this play was really performed in the Cathedral of Valencia, as in all probability it was (cf. Sanchis y Sivera, 8 and n. 1), the light which poured through the *linterna,* constructed as early as 1404, would have provided remarkable scenic effects for the Heaven constructed beneath it. (Cf. Lampérez y Romea, *Historia de la arquitectura cristiana española en la edad media,* 571.)
[65] P. 85—"deuall langell e quant langel sera dauant la maria . . .; Mérimée's use of the word "surgit" for the angel's entrance is scarcely accurate enough (*L'art dramatique,* 46). P. 88—"E la maria estigua agenollada *contemplant lo deuallament* del IHS E quant lo IHS será dauāt ella la maria uaia corrent abesar li los pes." Mérimée would place the whole scaffold, with all its settings "dans le choeur en vue du maitre-autel" (p. 49), which would be entirely inconsistent with the so frequently obvious concern, that the audience see and understand clearly the action of the play. If the stage were inside the choir, large parts of the audience in the transepts would fail to see at the very least some of the stations in Mary's pilgrimage.
[66] At the conclusion of the first day's performance, a stage. direction reads: "e meten la maria dauall lo cadafal. Etraguen la ymage e facen tot laltre offiici" [*sic*].

The multiple stage then for the Valencian Assumption play was set on a huge raised platform which was erected in front of the choir entrance. The platform extended out toward the high altar and laterally somewhat into the transepts. On it were placed at least five different settings, the central one elaborately fitted out as the Virgin's mansion. The others represented the tomb and the various places where the Virgin stopped during her pilgrimage. The space beneath the platform was unseen by the spectators but was used, as it was nearly two centuries later in Cervantes' *Numancia*,[67] both as the source of thunder and as a place of concealment. High above the stage proper a sixth setting represented Heaven. There the angels stayed, and from it an *araceli* was lowered at times. If in addition to all this, a section of the church floor itself beyond the platform was employed on the second day for the large groups of players in the processions,[68] we can visualize for this piece a theater of almost limitless extension.

The technique of the multiple stage as employed in the cathedral of Valencia in the fifteenth century was not restricted to representations of the Assumption theme. The performances of Nativity plays used exactly the same method. Except for differences inherent in the subject-matter, even details of the Nativity staging conformed to a remarkable degree with those found necessary for the Assumption play. Sanchis y Sivera described the Christmas production as follows: "Desde el coro, en la parte de la epístola hasta el púlpito, que estaba en el presbiterio, se construía un tablado de bastante consistencia, sobre el que se colocaba el establo de Betlem, dentro del cual hallábanse representados en figura

---

Among the *offici* may have been included the ascent of an image representing the Virgin's spirit. For the ascent on the second day, Mérimée imagined that the *araceli* carried aloft "un Christ et une vierge de carton" (*L'art dramatique*, 48). The stage direction merely says, "e entrensen secretamēt lo IHS e la maria. E soptosamēt hixqua la ara celi" (p. 91).

[67] See below, pp. 56 ff.

[68] One cannot accept Mérimée's idea (*L'art dramatique*, 50) that a *considerable* part of the action of the second day took place off the platform. The manuscript itself gives no such indication. But since it is concerned primarily with the rôle of the Virgin, it may be that the mass scenes were performed on the church floor.

la Virgen, San José y el Niño Jesús, . . . rodeados de ángeles. . . .
En sitio no muy apartado veíanse unas torres, simulando la Ciudad
sagrada, y en segundo término contemplábanse las figuras de todos
los profetas. . . . pastores y pastoras, aquellos en número de vein-
ticinco, unos en figura y otros de carne y hueso . . . ocupaban el
resto del tablado hasta cerca del establo. . . . Fuera del tablado, y
en el coro, hallábase el árbol del Paraíso con las figuras de Adán y
Eva, y encima de dicho árbol aparecía también el Niño Jesús, ro-
deado de serafines. En lo alto del cimborio colocábanse un lienzo
pintado que figuraba el cielo, y en la barandilla había veinticuatro
niños vestidos de ángel . . . Así todo dispuesto, á una señal con-
venida abríase el lienzo . . . y salía una paloma de madera cubierta
de plumas de papel, la que por medio de un mecanismo especial,
llegaba hasta el establo de Betlem despidiendo fuego. Luégo bajaba
un ángel con un lirio en la mano, ... "[69]

As in the Assumption play, a platform constituted the major
portion of the stage. It was built in front of the choir. Upon it
a multiple stage was arranged consisting of 1) a stable, 2) towers,
and 3) an undecorated location for the shepherds. The stage also
extended beyond the platform, with the Garden of Eden placed
in the choir. Eden again included the indispensable tree which was
used in the *Misteri de Adam y Eva.* Heaven was once more a
canopy in the dome which opened and closed. From it the *araceli*
lowered a dove and an angel. These numerous features which were
identical in the staging of two different themes suggest that the
multiple stage method was the regular system in the Cathedral
of Valencia. The text of the Assumption play is a lone, surviving
representative of what may well have been a flourishing and active
center of dramatic art.

Toward the close of the same century[70] the city of Elche was
being entertained annually in the first *iglesia de Santa María* by

[69] *La dramática en nuestra catedral,* 3-4. This description is a synthesis of many
scattered items in the *Libre de obres* between 1429 and 1531.
[70] The date of the earliest form of the Elche Assumption play has been variously placed, before 1492 by Milá y Fontanals (*Obras,* VI, 221) and by Bonilla (*Las
bacantes,* 78), and after 1492 by Vidal y Valenciano (Milá, *Obras,* VI, 338). Both

another two-day Assumption play, which, with slight but significant modifications, is the same play as the Valencian piece.[71] This later version is shorter, a little less complicated in action, and much less encumbered with large unwieldy groups of characters. It was performed on a multiple stage which contained the same settings[72] as the Valencian play, and which closely followed it in the order and arrangement of the action. A marked difference obtained, however, in the distribution of the settings, and a greater development in the form and use of aerial machinery is evident.

The action has been spread at the very beginning to include ap-

these datings have been discredited by the enthusiastic acceptance by Mérimée (L'art dramatique, 51) of Felipe Pedrell's demonstration that some of the music cannot have antedated the first half of the sixteenth century (La festa d'Elche, 203-252). Yet Pedrell himself, with the complete agreement of his able reviewer M. Rouanet (RHi, VIII [1901], 540-542), has indicated that our earliest known version is at least two steps away from the original. Even the present textual form, however, containing St. Thomas' final remark about the Indies (Milá, Obras, VI, 347), must date the play near the year of their discovery. An undoubted sixteenth century auto contains the same reference (Rouanet, Colección, II, Num. XXXII, 253-254), and the apostle had been associated with India at least as early as the apocryphal Acts of Thomas. But one cannot escape the conviction that the development of St. Thomas as a comic character, with his topical allusion to a newly discovered land, probably began in or shortly after the year 1492. Pedrell himself assumes that the original play dates "du commencement du XVIe siècle" (p. 29). It is significant that the two earlier Assumption plays, which both antedate Columbus' epoch-making voyage, contain no rôle for St. Thomas and no allusion, comic or serious, to his preaching in the Indies. This is particularly significant when we realize that the Catalonian play contains such textual similarities and identities with the Elche play as to lead Pedrell to call it the source and inspiration of the later piece (pp. 40, n. 2 and 45). Now the development of the rôle of St. Thomas, which has attained considerable proportions in the sixteenth century auto, is scarcely more than embryonic in the Misterio de Elche, where it is accorded a single short speech and that at the very end of the play. It seems like the beginning of a new rôle in the Assumption theme— a new note which we think must have been introduced soon after 1492. The content and structure, if not the music, of the play as we now have it, although in an early sixteenth century dress, could then date back to that year.

[71] The text is printed in Milá, Obras, VI, 341-347. Admitting the similarity in scenic method, Mérimée holds that the two are not the same play at all, because the tone of the Valencian work is serious and reverent while in the Elche Assumption "domine la note populaire" (L'art dramatique, 53). The entrance and speeches of St. Thomas support Mérimée's characterization, but its chief prop is removed when we discover that the judiada did not always occur in the Elche performances as Mérimée thought. This episode did occur, however, in later versions (Alcahalí, 67; Milá, Obras, VI, 219; Pedrell, 19 ff.). Pedrell insists that in any case the popular note is characteristic only of the second part (p. 15). Cf. also Corbató, "Notas sobre El Misterio de Elche y otros dramas sagrados de Valencia," in Hispania, XV (1932), 103, 106. Part of the judiada was omitted in 1931 and "the suppressions of the episode . . . must be of ancient date" (Ratcliff, "The Mystery of Elche in 1931," in Hispania, XV [1932], 111, 112, 114-115).

[72] One stop in the pilgrimage, the Mount of Olives, was omitted, and another location, undecorated and unnamed, was added.

parently the entire church as its stage. The Virgin enters the church, stops and kneels "en medio del corredor," "pasa un poco más adelante y arrodillada ante el huerto," breaks out into a lament. She stops further on "enfrente de la cruz" and "pasa al Sepulcro," until she finally "Sube . . . al tablado" and kneels "sobre su rica cama."[73] Only one of these settings appeared on the platform itself, and the importance of the platform has therefore diminished. The modern version played at Elche, using the nave as the *corredor,* placing the *tablado* in the crossing, and decorating certain columns with the symbols of Gethsemane, Calvary and the tomb, must not vary much in structure from the original.[74]

Later the first day when the apostles join Mary, we read, "Entran los Apóstoles y suben al tablado, excepto tres de ellos, que quedándose en el corredor, cantan."[75] Thus a section of the open nave itself afforded an additional location off the scaffold, and one which was in active use at the same time as the very house of the Virgin. Another and similar use of this unnamed location occurred at the opening of the second day's performance when "Entran los apóstoles y Marías, éstas se quedan en el corredor . . ." (p. 345 SD).

Heaven and its machines were somewhat more highly developed than in the earlier Valencian version. For the angel's descent, the stage direction says, "sale del cielo una dorada nube, y abriéndose aparece en medio de ella un Angel . . ." (p. 342 SD). After his duties are performed the angel departs "elevándose hacia el cielo," and when he arrives, "Se cierra la nube, desaparece el Angel . . ." (p. 342 SD's). A second time on the first day and just before the end, "Ábrese de repente el cielo, y sale el Aracoeli" (p. 344 SD), which carries aloft the Virgin, now represented by the image, the final direction reading, "Entra en el cielo el alma de la Virgen . . ."

---

[73] Milá, *Obras,* VI, 341. The *cama* is once called a *tálamo* (p. 346 SD), which is undoubtedly symbolic rather than descriptive.

[74] Vidal y Valenciano (in Milá, *Obras,* VI, 326). Cf. also Alcahalí, 64-68, Pedrell, 6 ff., and Ratcliff, 110-11.

[75] Milá, *Obras,* VI, p. 343 SD: Pedrell's analysis (p. 11) agrees.

(p. 345 SD). The Aracoeli descends again the second day, again takes up an image of the Virgin, and as the apparatus arrives at its destination, "sale la Trinidad del cielo a recibir a esta señora, que acompañada de Angeles va elevándose" (pp. 346-347 SD). The upper level equipment in the performance of this play consisted then of three distinct elements: first, a heaven with a door which opened and closed and which was located in the dome of the church;[76] second, a golden cloud which carried an actor, had also the mechanism for opening and closing, and which issued from the doorway of the heaven; and third, the familiar Aracoeli which must have appeared rich indeed, for St. Thomas sees "en lo alto *el resplandeciente solio* en que sube la Virgen." Possibly the Trinity also descended part way on another machine or second Aracoeli to meet the Virgin Mary as she rose.[77]

On the second day the tomb was probably on the platform also, for the Aracoeli descended, as we have seen, to receive the spirit of the Virgin. The nature of the tomb is obscure. A stage direction reads: "toman los Apóstoles la Imagen y la llevan con gran solemnidad bajo del Palio . . . y después la dan sepultura" (p. 346 SD's). Perhaps it was merely a hole in the platform, as it was in 1931,[78] into which the *Aracoeli* was lowered bodily.

In such a case a lower level compartment beneath the platform would have been used. Furthermore a *Consueta* of 1639 which treats the same theme says, " 'Dans le tombeau doivent se trouver des personnes habiles, pour savoir donner l'image aux anges.' "[79] Even if a low tomb appeared above the stage level, additional space below must have been required for such stage business.

The staging of the Elche Assumption play modified the Valencian method in two important respects. The settings which repre-

---

[76] Cf. Pedrell, 6. Nowadays there is only a hole six feet square in the canvas Heaven (Ratcliff, 110) for the ancient practicable door.

[77] Milá, *Obras*, VI, p. 347 SD. See Alcahalí, 62, 68, as well as "La fête de l'Assomption à Elche," in *l'Illustration*, Sept. 18, 1897, for pictures of modern counterparts of the cloud and the *aracoeli*. Today three different objects are lowered from Heaven by means of trapezes—a pomegranate carrying the angel, the *araceli*, and the mechanism which lowers the Holy Trinity (Ratcliff, 110-113).

[78] Ratcliff, 110-113.

[79] Pedrell, 24.

sented the places of Christ's torture and which were stopping points in the Virgin's pilgrimages were not erected on the platform. In the Valencian play some action doubtless took place off the platform; in the Elche performances stage decoration as well as dramatic action was spread out through the church. The stage was larger and its limits less precise than in the earlier Assumption plays. In the second place, the function of Heaven in the development of the play was more important. Two or three machines instead of one operated from the doorway of Heaven. Singly or in combination they raised and lowered living figures.

Regarding the multiple stage before the sixteenth century the following conclusions may be suggested on the basis of the limited material available:

The antiquity of the multiple stage in Spain is at least as great as the earliest records of staging methods. Before 1399 we know nothing of either. From that year on, both elaborate stage scenery and the multiple technique definitely existed, frequently together. A dramatic performance once started tended to endure and become traditional. The three Valencian mysteries on St. Christopher, Adam and Eve, and Herod persisted until well into the seventeenth century.[80] The Elche Assumption play, begun toward the end of the century, survives to the present day.[81]

The earliest known multiple stages were already highly developed. The celebration of 1399, with its Heaven and its rising and falling cloud, included an upper level of the type that was employed throughout the following century. And the Catalonian Assumption play of 1420 or earlier was performed on an elaborate one-level stage with five mansions. Unless the system was transferred suddenly and bodily from France, it must have gone through

[80] Corbató, 75-77.
[81] Many other less famous but similar modern survivals of ancient religious dramatic performances might be observed throughout Spain. Cf. e.g., Llabrés, "Un hallazgo literario interesante," in *BSAL*, 10 abril de 1887, p. 53 b; ———, "Repertorio de 'Consuetas' representadas en las iglesias de Mallorca (siglos XV y XVI)," in *RABM*, V (1901), 926 n. 1; Juliá Martínez, "Representaciones teatrales de carácter popular en la provincia de Castellón," in *BRAE*, XVII (1930), 97-112; Rodríguez, "El teatro religioso de Gómez Manrique," in *RyC*, XXIX (1935), 87 n. 2, 94.

an adolescent period to achieve such maturity. It may be inferred that some elementary or embryonic form of simultaneous staging existed in the fourteenth century and possibly even in the thirteenth.

In the fifteenth century the multiple stage technique was employed chiefly in Eastern Spain. Catalonian and Valencian plays were performed with simultaneous settings, and in the Cathedral of Valencia and multiple stage may have been the usual method. A vertical multiple stage was early used in Zaragoza, and toward the end of the century in Seville. In the second half of the century a simple form of multiple stage on one level appeared in Castile, as the Jaen Nativity performance shows. If Castilian texts should be discovered, it might turn out that the method was not so generally restricted to Eastern Spain as it now seems.

The multiple stage provided a method of performance primarily for religious plays. Its highest development appeared in productions inside the church. It seems, furthermore, to have been almost, if not absolutely, the exclusive system during this early period. The only exceptions were the simplest and least pretentious dramatic offerings, such as the Castilian *momos* and possibly tableaux or simple pantomimic shows without dialogue on some of the Valencian *rocas*. The *Misteri de San Christofol* cannot properly be considered an exception since it is incomplete.

Two levels for Earth and Heaven were employed in the Zaragoza and Barcelona celebrations, the Seville Corpus festival, the Colometa ceremony, the Valencian Nativity performances, and in four of the seven plays discussed: the *Misteri de Adam y Eva,* the Valencian and Elche Assumption plays, and the Majorcan play on the Temptation. The subjects of two plays do not require a heaven (Herod, St. Christopher). Only the Catalonian Assumption placed Heaven (called *Paradis*) on the same level as the other settings.

The Elche and Valencian Assumption plays required a substage compartment. Noises and smoke were produced in it and it provided a hiding place for actors and assistants. The interior of the compartment was unseen by the spectators and cannot properly be called a lower level section of the stage. A horizontal multiple stage was employed by nearly all the plays. All three Assumption plays used at least five mansions or settings on the same stage level. The Valencian and Elche performances may possibly have involved more than five. The Valencian Nativity play used four locations, three of which were settings. The stage for the Jaen Epiphany celebration contained at least two locations, one of them equipped with setting. The Catalonian Temptation utilized two platforms besides an undecorated location and the presumably raised platform for Heaven. Two locations and one setting (*portalet*) were needed for the Herod mystery, and possibly one location besides the Garden of Eden setting for the Adam and Eve play. Thus, while the number of settings and locations varied from play to play, no performance can definitely be said to have employed an Earth level that was provided by a simple, single, one-location stage. The only possible exceptions are those ceremonies like the *Colometa* for which texts are lacking. For them it is impossible to reconstruct a complete picture.

A setting for Hell appeared only in the two Catalonian plays—a mansion in the *Asumpció* and a platform in the *Tentatio*. Both were built on the Earth level. And the setting for Heaven in these two plays was fundamentally different from that of all the others. It was a mansion on the Earth level in the *Asumpció* and a high platform in the *Tentatio*. In all the other performances—the Zaragoza and Barcelona pageants, the Seville Corpus celebration, the Valencian Nativity and Adam and Eve plays, and the Assumptions of Valencia and Elche—Heaven was a canopy suspended from above. It was reached in all seven cases by trapeze-like machines, the *araceli* or a cloud.

The settings on Earth were many in number and varied in nature. At least eight places of action were represented by decoration. Several others, which have tentatively been called locations (the "world" in the *Misteri de Adam y Eva;* the wheat field in the Herod mystery; the Mount of Olives in the Valencian Assumption; and unnamed places in the Valencian Nativity, the Herod mystery, the Majorcan *Tentatio,* and the Elche Assumption) may also have been decorated. A mountain was represented by a double scaffold (*Tentatio*) ; the Holy City by towers (Valencian Nativity) ; the Jews' cabin by a beautiful synagogue or council hall (Catalonian Assumption) ; and the stations of the Virgin's pilgrimage by representative objects like the tomb and the cross (Valencian and Elche Assumption plays). A low flat box-like structure evidently represented the tomb for the Virgin in all three Assumption plays.

The Virgin's mansion in these plays was erected upon a platform. It contained a bed and seems to have resembled a house or room, for it had an entrance door (Catalonian Assumption, Valencian Assumption) with a knocker (Valencian Assumption). Inside the room there was also a chair (Valencian Asumption). In one play (Catalonian Assumption) the bed was curtained off and a chapel was annexed to the house.

The Garden of Eden was decorated with the inevitable tree (Adam and Eve mystery, Valencian Nativity) and sometimes with other foliage and fruit (Adams and Eve mystery). The Nativity setting varied from a chair in the simple Castilian performance at Jaen to a doorway with a grating in the Herod play and something similar (*establo*) in the Valencian Nativity.

The Catalonian plays most faithfully preserve the multiple stage system as it was practiced north of the Pyrenees. Both the *Assumpció* and the *Tentatio* employed mansions or settings that were definitely allocated to particular characters in the plays. An actor went to his mansion at the beginning of the play and would return to it after any part of the action had taken him away from it. Furthermore Heaven was, like the French *Paradis,* a mansion on the Earth level (*Asumpció*) or on a platform raised above this level (*Tentatio*).

The other early performances in Spain did not adhere so closely to this conception of the mansion, and in them Heaven was an utterly different setting. On the Earth level, one setting was more elaborately decorated and was more important to the action than the others. In the Nativity plays and the Herod mystery it was the Bethlehem or manger setting, in the *Misteri de Adam y Eva* the Garden of Eden, and in the Assumption plays the Virgin's mansion. Whether this illustrates a tendency toward a simple stage is not altogether clear. For in the Valencian and Elche Assumption plays fully as many additional settings appeared as were used for any multiple stage in the entire group. Besides, the size of the whole stage was so large as to include practically the entire church. The relative emphasis on one setting in all these plays does illustrate, however, a definite variation from the Catalonian and French system, and possibly a modification of that system.

CHAPTER II

THE VERTICAL MULTIPLE STAGE IN THE SIXTEENTH CENTURY

I. HEAVEN AND THE UPPER LEVEL

The chief fifteenth century methods for a scenic representation of Heaven were followed in the sixteenth. Both the high scaffold of the Temptation play and the suspended canopy of the other dramatic works continued to be used. The sixteenth century also saw abundant use of the *araceli*, which usually accompanied the canopy Heaven, and also of other forms of aerial machinery. Even the unelevated mansion of the Catalonian *Asumpció* may have had a successor in *La representació del deuallar del infern*.[1] Toward the close of this short piece Christ says to a group including Adam, Eve and Abraham,

> "Veniu ab mi e dar vos he
> tot lo que promes vos he;
> entrarem en paradis terrenal
> hont es lo pare celestial."

The stage direction which follows this speech says they are "prop lo paradis" (1087 SD), and the play soon ends when all "entraran dins" (1099 SD). The position of this setting relative to the Earth level can only be imagined. But at least there is no indication whatever that it was raised above the rest of the stage.

The only known representation of Heaven by a high scaffold occurs in the Majorcan *Consueta del Juy*.[2] A long prose introduction carefully describes the arrangement of the stage as follows: "Per recitar la present Consueta se fara un cadefal gran quan pora en la capella mes el mig de la Iglesia, algun tant enfora, y detras dell sen fara un altre iunt a nel mateix ques puge de un

---

[1] Pub. by Durán i Sanpere, "Un misteri de la Passió a Cervera," in *Estudis universitaris catalans*, VII (1913), 241 ff., lines 1012-1099. For further discussion of the performances and the stage for this play, see below, pp. 51, 77.
[2] Pub. by Llabrés, in *RABM*, VI (1902-1), 456-466.

40

al altre" (p. 456). After directing that chairs and musical instruments be placed on the upper platform, the text says that Jesus, Mary and a group of saints "puiran . . . el cadefal mes alt" (p. 456). Although Earth was also placed on a platform, the scaffold for Heaven was higher. This form of staging shows an attempt at verisimilitude in the representation of the vertical relationship between Heaven and Earth, if not in the scenic decoration of the two levels.

This kind of raised setting, apparently rare in the representation of Heaven, was widely used for other purposes. An elevated part of the stage was sometimes used to represent the scenery for a window, a balcony, or a wall.[3] A kind of elevation for a hill or rock may have been employed as early as the *Auto o Farsa del Nascimiento de Nuestro Señor Jesucristo* of Lucas Fernández.[4] Many other examples would show similar use of a raised portion of the stage.[5] Each of these places may have been represented on the stage by a scaffold, a raised platform, or some arrangement of trestles. The resultant mansion may have looked like the Heaven of the *Consueta del Juy*. The essential difference lay in the imaginary distance between the elevated mansion and the lower settings. When the former represented Heaven the distance was infinite; when it represented a hill or wall the distance may have been little more than the few feet that actually separated the places of action. In both cases, of course, the mansion rose structurally from the main part of the stage.

An upper-level canopy provided the usual decoration, however, for the representation of Heaven in the sixteenth century. The texts of several plays amply illustrate the persistence of fifteenth century methods in this respect. With the possible exception of the *Representación de los mártires Justo y Pastor*, these plays do

---

[3] Cf. Shoemaker, "Windows on the Spanish Stage in the Sixteenth Century," in *HR*, II (1934), 303-318.
[4] *Farsas y Églogas*, pub. by Cañete, Madrid, 1867, 192-194.
[5] See, e.g., in addition to those given by Shoemaker, p. 313, the *peña* in Cervantes' *Numancia* (*Obras completas*, pub. by Schevill and Bonilla, Vol. 5, Madrid, 1920, p. 107, line 6 SD).

not seem to have advanced beyond the earlier technique. But their number shows its extension and increased popularity.

In an *Aucto de la Asuncion de Nuestra Señora*,[6] the appearance and the function of Heaven and its machines seem to be as elaborate as in the earlier Elche play, of which this *auto* is probably a descendant.[7] At the death of the Virgin, "Aqui se abre el cielo, y parescen las tres personas de la Trenidad, cantando con el anima" (141 SD). After the interlude of the Jews, "Luego se abr'el çielo, y baja el anima con un coro de angeles, y dize Dios Padre . . ." (211 SD). After a brief dialogue "Sube el cuerpo" while again "Cantan las personas de la Trenidad" (226 SD), and "Llegada arriba, la coronan todas tres personas" (226 SD). The crowning is accompanied by a short speech by God the Father and the songs of the Angels to their Empress and Queen. In the lengthened St. Thomas epilogue, a final gesture from the upper level occurs when "le hechan del cielo la çinta de Nuestra Señora (272 SD).

In the performance of this play the setting for Heaven was evidently the overhead canopy. It was equipped with a doorway or entrance which could be opened and closed. When it was open, Heaven became the stage for the action of the play, involving pantomime and music as well as dialogue. Although not specifically named, the *araceli* seems to have served as the means of ascent and descent.

The position, use and appearance of Heaven in this Assumption play was identical in another *auto* on the same subject, so far as can be judged from its present fragmentary form. At the death of the Virgin, "se abre el çielo, y cantan Dios padre y los angeles."[8] In the *Aucto de los Triunfos de Petrarca (a lo divino)*, Heaven is used as the location for a veritable Deus ex machina. The struggles and contentions of a host of allegorical but worldly characters are suddenly terminated when "abrese una nuve donde paresçe

---

[6] Rouanet, *Colección*, II, Num. XXXII, 8-20.
[7] The *auto* even includes the comic rôle of St. Thomas and the once topical reference to the Indies.
[8] Rouanet, *Colección*, II, Num. XXXI, pp. 1-7, 136 SD.

Xpo con sus angeles cantando."[9] Afterwards our Savior speaks several times without moving from his aerial location. The upper level is similarly used in the *Aucto de la Paciencia de Job*.[10] Early in the text appears the direction, "Aquí le llama [a Satan] Dios Padre desde una nuve (30), twice repeated later in the play (256 SD, 556 SD). And from the ninth *Coloquio* of González de Eslava, where "Aparece una nube en lo alto, y abrese, y aparece dentro de ella la Justicia,"[11] it is evident that the upper-level Heaven had passed to Mexico.

The same kind of setting for Heaven may be inferred for the performance of a third *Auto de la Asumption de Nuestra Señora*. A brief stage direction proves the use of the *araceli* as in the other Assumption plays: " . . . y enpieça a subir el cuerpo."[12] Now, as we have seen, every other fifteenth and sixteenth century Assumption play that used the *araceli* employed an elaborate, upper-level Heaven also. It is, therefore, highly probable that in this *auto* the usual setting appeared up above.[13] Furthermore, in plays on other subjects also, when the *araceli* was employed a setting for Heaven usually appeared. Such a setting may be inferred then also for a performance of the *Aucto de Sant Francisco*. At the end of the play a stage direction reads: "Aqui suben el anima los Angeles al *cielo*."[14] The use of a machine such as the *araceli* is thus definitely indicated and Heaven is specifically mentioned.

A different use of aerial machinery appears in Ferruz's *Auto*

[9] Rouanet, *Colección*, II, Num. LVIII, pp. 479-501, 560 SD.
[10] Rouanet, *Colección*, IV, Num. XCVI, 105-127.
[11] Ed. García Icazbalceta, p. 118.
[12] Rouanet, *Colección*, III, Num. LXII, pp. 19-33, 414.
[13] San Juan and Santiago watched the body as it rose. The last words of Santiago's comment suggest that singers were stationed aloft:
   "Sus, hermanos! que hazemos?   (422)
   con las celest(r)es quadrillas
   nuestro cantico entonemos."
[14] Rouanet, *Colección*, II, Num. XXXIX, 110-132, line 670 SD. An earlier flight on the *araceli* seems to be indicated by line 62 SD, "Aqui buelve San Francisco qu'estava elevado." Whatever may be the exact significance of this, it is evident that considerably more scenery and properties were required than the stage directions explicitly show.

de Cain y Abel and in the *Cortes de la Muerte* by Micael de Carvajal and Luis Hurtado de Toledo. In the former "Baja el fuego sobre el sacrificio de Abel, y no sobr'el de Cayn."[15] The machine that descended may have been a trapeze resembling the *araceli,* but it fulfilled quite a different purpose. In the *Cortes de la Muerte* "bajará una nube con dos ángeles y dos trompetas."[16] Here *nube* is not merely a variant term for *cielo* or Heaven itself as in the *Triunfos de Petrarca* and the *Paciencia de Job,* but the transporting machine or moving *tramoya* itself. It may have resembled the cloud used in the Elche Assumption, where it appeared in addition to the *araceli.*

Whether or not a setting for Heaven formed part of the stage decoration in these two plays is not clear. Since Heaven is neither mentioned nor used in the action, the decoration may have been left to the imagination of the spectators, as was often the case when a star moved across the sky[17] or angels flew through the air.[18] The number of such mechanical tricks to dazzle and amaze the audience could be increased by examples of flying birds, both real and artificial.[19] Indeed these *tramoyas* (machines) constituted

[15] Rouanet, *Colección,* II, Num. XLI (pp. 150-166), 95 SD. Cf. Mérimée, *L'art dramatique,* 231. In the early seventeenth century descendant of Maestro Ferruz's play, the *Auto de los dos primeros hermanos* by Juan Caxes, the action of the *araceli* is required by the identical stage direction, "Baxa . . . Abel" (*RHi,* VIII [1901], 139 ff., line 1072).

[16] *BAE,* XXXV, 3b SD.

[17] The Portuguese *Auto do Nascimento* of Baltasar Diaz (Carolina Michaëlis, *Autos portugueses*) best illustrates a continuance of this device in the sixteenth century. After the entrance of the wise men, "Aqui aparece hum Anjo & a estrela, & fala o Anjo dôde estaa a estrella, . . ." ([Axj], verso, SD) and "Yrão os tres Reis magos cõ a estrela diante desi q̃ osguia cantando, & chegando onde estara feyto Hierusalem desaparecera a estrela . . ." ([Axij], recto, SD), at which Belchior comments that they can no longer see "o ceo claro." When the Kings leave Herod, "tornarlhe ha aparecer a Estrella" ([Axiij], verso, SD) to guide them to Bethlehem.

[18] Continuing old and anticipating later custom, Cueva's *Comedia del Viejo Enamorado,* performed in the Corral de Don Juan at Seville, included the flight through the air of the four Furies and Arcelo (*Comedias y Tragedias,* Madrid, 1917, II, pp. 318, 327, 340). Whether the angel in Aparicio's *El Pecador* actually moved through the air or was merely imagined to be doing so off stage is not clear (Gallardo, *Ensayo,* I, Num. 216, p. 236 Dialogue).

[19] Ricardo del Arco, drawing from the Archives of the cathedral at Huesca, records that there was an expense item of "treinta sueldos por doce palomas se husaron (*sic*) en dicha Pascua [de Resurreccion de 1591]" ("Misterios, autos sacramentales y otras fiestas en la catedral de Huesca," in *RABM,* XLI [1920], 267), This may indeed again refer to the old ceremony known as the Palometa (cf. above, pp. 14-15). In regard to an anonymous sixteenth century Christmas play Alenda

a major contribution of the early theater to performances in the seventeenth century *corrales*.[20] With all the abundant evidence of the existence and use of an upper-level Heaven we would nevertheless be considerably handicapped in attempting an accurate reconstruction for any given play, were it not for the manuscript of Francisco de las Cuebas' *Representación de los mártires Justo y Pastor*.[21] Preceding Act II a long preliminary stage direction appears which describes in detail certain material features of the staging. Concerning Heaven it says, " . . . se representó cómo baxaron los Angeles del cielo . . . y cómo Jesu Xpo los recibió con gran música y alegría de los coros angelicales; para lo qual se hizo un arco grande de treinta y seis pies en alto, y veinte y ocho en medio; en medio del cual se hizo un zielo que tenia quatorze pies en güeco y en ancho diez, y siete pies en largo. Este se governaba por de dentro y hazia su arco y daba sus vueltas como el verdadero cielo. Auia musica de dentro y gente. Tenia sus puertas zerradas, las cuales se abrian con estrellas de oro de que toda la mitad estaba quajado. Esto era á la parte donde estaba la luna, porque la otra mitad donde estaba el sol, solamente tenia su color azul. Este se hizo de lienzo, fundado

---

states that in the third act "El Pueblo Hebreo remedia un hambre pública haciendo caer aves del cielo" ("Catálogo," in *BRAE*, VI [1919], 763). The lowering of a *cuervo* with bread in its mouth occurred in the *Aucto de la Visitaçion de Sant Antonio a Sant Pablo* (Rouanet, *Colección*, III, Num. LXXVI, 261-275, line 187 SD, etc.).

[20] Alonso López Pinciano wrote in 1596: "porque ay vnas q̃ conuienen para vn milagro, y otras para otro diferente, y tienen sus differencias segun las personas, porque el Angel ha de parecer que buela, y el santo que anda por el ayre, los pies juntos, el vno y el otro que descienden de alto, y el demonio que sube de abaxo" (*Philosophia antigva poetica*, 523). Cf. also Schack, II, 265; Buchanan, 208. According to the Countess d'Aulnoy's account of her imaginary visit to Spain, the celestial figures sometimes appeared "en una viga, que se extiende de un extremo a otro del teatro" (Schack, II, 249). Although the French lady's *voyage* never took place, so reputable does Foulché-Delbosc judge the sources of her information, that her account loses little of its value as a faithful chronicle of conditions in the last years of the seventeenth century (*RHi*, LXVII [1926], 90 ff.). But private and special performances, if not those in the *corrales*, continued the elaborate scenic technique developed in the preceding centuries. An example of this is found in the ceremonies attendant upon the baptism of Philip IV in a *sala* of the palace at Valladolid on May 29, 1605. A *cielo* was made at one end of the *sala*, and from it a *nube* was repeatedly lowered and raised (*Relacion del Bautismo de Felipe IV*, pub. by Narciso Alonso Cortés with his translation of Tomé Pinheiro da Veiga, *Fastiginia o Fastos Geniales*, pp. 38-39).

[21] Pub. by Crawford, in *RHi*, XIX (1908), 431-453.

en aros de zedazos Estaba en dos medios, porque de otra suerte no se podia hazer bien. Estaba fundado cada medio en dos medias lunas de madera, de las quales iban muchas riostras á todas las partes de los arcos, porque de otra manera, no pudiera tener firmeza. Encajaronse estas dos medias lunas en una gruesa viga redonda y larga que atrabesaba todo el arco en medio; en medio de la qual viga, se hizo un andamio donde pudiese estar la gente que estaba dentro del dicho cielo. Tenia este cielo por un lado una puerta pequeña, á la qual cubrian dos Angeles que estaban gouernando el cielo de la una parte, y otros dos de la otra, y por ella entraban y salían; por lo qual era necesario, sin que persona lo viese."[22]

This Heaven may not be typical or representative of sixteenth century practices. Its great size and its gala appearance may not always have been equalled in other performances. Other Heavens may not all have been made of colored cloth, constructed under a huge arch, and adorned with stars and sun and moon. All of them probably did not revolve, nor did they have a hidden door.

On the other hand, this Heaven should not be considered such an extreme exception or variation from the other Heavens as might at first be supposed. Three reasons may be suggested in support of this view. In the first place, there is no other document of either the fifteenth or the sixteenth century with which to compare the *Justo y Pastor* manuscript. Other documents and texts afford but partial descriptions, which, in the sixteenth century especially, are very brief and are confined largely to describing how the setting for Heaven was used. The text of the *Justo y Pastor* play is truly exceptional in recording a detailed description of Heaven.[23] But this does not necessarily mean that such a setting

[22] *RHi*, XIX, 440.
[23] At Barcelona in 1500, "Ibi effictum coelum relucebat," and at Perpignan a "paradisus . . . mero artificio constructa" contained machines for firing rockets (Schack, I, 326 n. 1). But we do not know what these machines looked like.
An approximation to the description in the *Justo y Pastor* text may be found in the early seventeenth century *Auto de los desposorios de la Virgen* by Juan Caxes. In this play, after Joseph has fallen asleep, "Aqui del Arca de Noe que estara hecha en la fachada del carro se levantara en alto una nube y saldra un arco con los atributos de la Virgen, y ella en medio en un trono sobre la luna y el dragon a

for Heaven was unique. In the second place, many of the features of the *Justo y Pastor* Heaven had long before been recorded separately. The cloth material, the stars and the sun, and the revolving movement have all been briefly noted earlier.[24] Finally, the functions of this Heaven are precisely the ones observed in other Heavens. Human bodies representing angels ascended and descended. The setting for Heaven opened and closed, permitting them to pass through. By means of its platform (*andamio*) it was able to accommodate both actors and musicians. Now, these functional characteristics are repeated in the stage directions as follows: "A este tiempo se abrió el cielo y sonó mucha música y se vieron venir angeles y subir las animas al cielo, en el qual se cantó este villancico . . . Aqui llegaron las almas á lo alto y se boluió a zerrar el cielo . . . "[25] But these are the only characteristics of the setting for Heaven afforded by the stage directions. If, therefore, we were limited to the stage directions, as we are in the study of other plays, we should be forced to conclude that the setting for Heaven in the *Justo y Pastor* play was thoroughly typical.

In view of these facts, the Heaven of the *Justo y Pastor* play is not an exception but a confirmation of all the other evidence of an upper-level Heaven in the sixteenth century. It may have been more elaborate than others, but it did not vary from the general type. The long and detailed preliminary notice complements the information presented by the stage directions in the texts of all the plays, including the *Justo y Pastor* itself. The notice substantiates the fact that in the representation of Heaven the sixteenth century stage builders indulged in a highly developed technique.

---

los pies. . . ., y el cielo que se levante se pinte de sol, luna y estrellas." (*RHi*, VIII (1901), 173, line 648 SD). Agreeing with Rouanet (*RHi*, VIII (1901), 93, 96), A. Restori says, "aun en la técnica del arte teatral . . . [Caxes] nos parece buen medianero entre los autos primitivos [Auto Num. 94 of the Rouanet collection, for example] y la manera de Lope" (*RHi*, IX (1902), 357).

[24] See above, pp. 13-16, etc.

[25] P. 446. These are also substantially the facts recorded by Morales in his account of the performance (see below, p. 116 n. 155). He calls the *cielo* a *nube* (fols. 122r, 135v, 141v, etc.).

This technique was a heritage from the fifteenth century[26] and conformed in general, if not in all details, to fifteenth century practice in France and Italy.[27] A Heaven (*cielo* or *nube*) was constructed at some distance above the Earth level, usually with an opening in it, through which actors or images could be lowered and raised, either on an apparatus resembling a cloud or on the *araceli*.

II. HELL AND THE LOWER LEVEL

Hell was not a favorite setting in Spanish staging. It appeared in the sixteenth century only a little more often than in the fifteenth. Whatever material form it took, the interior seems not to have been revealed to the spectators. The part of Hell which therefore received most attention was the entrance, which must, at times, have been very impressive indeed.[28]

The infrequency of Hell as a dramatic setting is suggested not only by the paucity and brevity of available descriptions but by its rare use in the dramatic texts as a place of action. In the texts Hell is sometimes off stage. In the *Auto de Cain y Abel*[29] Ynbidia refers to Hell as Satan's cave (*cueva*) and announces her intention of going there (166-170). She leaves the stage immediately after this remark.[30] In the *Aucto de Acusacion contra el Genero Humano*[31] Lucifer's exhortation, "Entremos en el ynfier-

[26] It is obvious that the statement of Cervantes that Navarro invented *nubes* in the sixteenth century ("Prologo," 7, lines 10-11; cf. also below, p. 57) was incorrect.

[27] Cohen, 82-84; D'Ancona, I, 282.

[28] That part of Hell called Limbo was employed by the sixteenth century drama perhaps more often than Hell proper. The scenic representation of this temporary dwelling place of unredeemed souls, was usually limited also to an entrance (see below, pp. 87-88). Crawford says that in the *Aucto de la Redencion del Genero Humano* (Rouanet, *Colección*, IV, 47 ff.), "Hell is represented as a medieval fortress" ("The Devil as a Dramatic Figure in the Spanish Religious Drama before Lope de Vega," in *RR*, I (1910), 375). But the verses which seem to describe Hell in this way must be only a poetic metaphor for the strength and impregnability of Satan's home. For this play is merely the final *auto* of Palau's *Victoria Christi*, where Hell is really Limbo, probably represented by the choir. The choir entrance can very well be the *puertas* referred to in the text (*Aucto*, 472 SD; *Victoria Christi*, p. 36, recto, col. 2) and the only piece of scenery necessary to a performance of the act (see below, pp. 113-114, for my discussion of the *Victoria Christi*).

[29] Rouanet, *Colección*, II, Num. XLI, 150 ff.

[30] Ynbidia's exit is inferred from two facts: she takes no part in the subsequent dialogue for 185 lines, and her next participation in the dialogue is prefaced by a stage direction indicating her reappearance on the stage (355).

[31] Rouanet, *Colección*, II, Num. LVII, 449 ff.

no" (132) is immediately followed by his exit with Satan and Charon.[32] The dialogue of the *Aucto de la Culpa y Captividad*[33] is rather more descriptive of Hell, calling it a *cueva* (156, 171), and a *breñal de serpientes* (50) "so aquella peña" (234). But here also every time the actors enter Hell they leave the stage (95-97, 205-207).[34] If any decoration was used for this sort of off-stage Hell, probably little more than an entrance portal was shown on the stage.

Sometimes the entrance to Hell was the gaping mouth of a huge monster, doubtless the biblical Leviathan of the French *mystères*.[35] The accounts of the Cathedral of Huesca contain the following record, under *Expensa ordinaria,* for the Christmas celebrations of 1581 : "Iten á 15 de Enero de 1582, por mandato de los señores del Cabildo, di á su platero ciciliano ciento diez y seis sueldos para hacer *una boca de infierno* y unos vestidos y cetros y otras cosillas *para la representacion de la* noche de *Navidad. . . .*"[36] This scenic device was probably similar to the wooden dragon's head that belched forth living children at Jaen a century earlier,[37] and not unlike St. George's dragon in the Majorcan *consueta,*

"lo qual lanse per la boca
fames de foch fins el   cel
ouellas y bous derroca
ab alé pudent y cruel."[38]

[32] Lucifer and Charon take no further part in the play and Satan's reentrance is indicated by 225 SD.
[33] Rouanet, *Colección,* II, Num. XLV, 243 ff.
[34] There is no indication that these "caves" were other than purely imaginary. To a list of imaginary caves as representations of Hell may be added the *Farsa llamada custodia del hombre* of Bartolomé Palau (pub. by Rouanet), line 3481. For a discussion of the cave as a scenic device other than as a representation of Hell, see below, pp. 83-84. The only suggestion we have found of the application of the term *cueva* to a lower level compartment occurs in the ninth *Coloquio* of González de Eslava (ed. García Icazbalceta, pp. 113-124), where the entrance of Truth is indicated by the stage direction, "Abrese la tierra, y sale la Verdad," and to which the following reference is made by *Oir* in the next line of dialogue, "¿Quién sale por esta cueva?" (p. 118).
[35] Cf. Cohen, 92-99; D'Ancona, I, 478; Stuart, "The Stage Setting of Hell," 332-333.
[36] Schack, I, 383 n. 1; also Ricardo del Arco, "Misterios, autos sacramentales y otras fiestas en la catedral de Huesca," in *RABM,* XLI (1920), 263 ff.
[37] See above, p. 12.
[38] *BSAL,* 25 abril de 1889, p. 58b; see also p. 59a for further descriptive items. Cf. below, p. 83, for the multiple stage in this play.

And perhaps the Hell-mouth was as old in Spain as the canopy Heaven. In the festivities of 1399 at Zaragoza in connection with the coronation of Martin I, "una grande culebra . . . echava por la boca grandes llamas de fuego."[39] Other notices of stage decoration for Hell are less explicit. At Barcelona in 1500 "infernus horrendus conspiciebatur," according to the account of Hubert Thomas of Liège.[40] A sixteenth century manuscript in the Academy of History bears the record that "en Alcázar de Consuegra y en Yébenes tienen de costumbre que el día del Corpus Christi hacen un infierno, donde están los que son diablos."[41] A Twelfth Night celebration of 1539 in Mexico included an *auto* dealing with St. Francis. As it was being performed on a *montaña* resembling the Valencian *roca*, "tornaba luego el santo á proceder en el sermon, y salian unas hechiceras muy bien contrahechas . . . y como tambien estorbasen la predicacion, y no cesasen, venian tambien los demonios, y poníanlas en el infierno. De esta manera fueron representados y reprendidos algunos vicios en este auto. El infierno tenia una puerta falsa, por donde salieron los que estaban dentro ; y salidos los que estaban dentro, pusieronle fuego, el cual ardio tan espantosamente, que pareció que nadie se había escapado. . . ."[42]

The nature of the setting for Hell at Barcelona is quite vague. The word *horrendus* suggests, however, that the Leviathan mouth may have been used. The Alcázar de Consuegra, Yébenes, and Mexican notices indicate that Hell was a mansion, where actors were placed. In all these cases, however, the interior of Hell was not necessarily visible. Indeed the use of the "puerta falsa" of the Mexican Hell proves that, for that performance at least, the audience could not see inside the mansion. Whether the setting for Hell in these instances had the huge mouth at the entrance is uncertain.

[39] Milá, *Obras*, VI, 237. The *tarascas* of the Corpus processions were the descendants of this infernal beast (cf. Sánchez-Arjona, *Anales*, 8; also Valbuena, 243, Fig. 63).
[40] Schack, I, 326 n. 1.
[41] *Cuentos de Garibay*, pub. by Paz y Mélia, *Sales Españolas*, II, 38.
[42] García Icazbalceta, xxi.

The manuscript of the Majorcan *Consueta del Juy*[43] affords the most complete account available of the appearance and dramatic use of Hell. A prose introduction carefully explains the characteristics of the stage. After directing that two platforms be built, adjacent to each other but of different heights, the text continues: "En lo cadefal mes baix nos posara cossa ninguna: *baix dest cadefal, sis pora: hage vna boca de infern, sino, posar y han una cortina para tapar lo baix de dit cadefal. Lo tal loch sera lo infern*" (p. 456). Jesus, Mary and a group of saints "puiran . . . el cadefal mes alt" (p. 456); a large group including the seven deadly sins "tots deu se poseran en el cadefal mes baix" (p. 457).; and the three devils "*entreran de aquella boca dinfern o deuall la cortina*" (p. 457). At one point in the action, "ixen los diables de infern" (p. 460, col. I SD) and "sen pugen alt el cadefal mes baix" (p. 460, col. 2 SD).

The scanty information on Hell in the text of the *Representació del deuallar del infern*[44] agrees, as far as it goes, with the facts already adduced. At one point in this play, "Fentse Adam a la boca del infern" (1017 SD), and later "pendra lo Jhs. una cadena y pose la al coll de Llucifer, qui stara a la boca del infern" (1035 SD). After Christ tells Lucifer what He is going to do to him, "fara apares de lligarlo en lo infern" (1039 SD). This would seem to indicate that the tying of Lucifer inside Hell was not seen by the spectators.

These two plays confirm the conclusions to be drawn from the other items of information and add some new features to the appearance of Hell. The interior of Hell was not visible; Hell itself was, in fact, off stage; and the entrance was the mouth of the Leviathan. But in the *Consueta* an alternate type of entrance is suggested. For some unknown reason, perhaps the expense of construction, the author or stage director designated the curtain as a substitute for the mouth.

An additional significant feature of the *Consueta del Juy* has to

[43] Pub. by Llabrés, in *RABM*, VI (1902-1), 456-466.
[44] Cf. above, p. 40.

do with the position of Hell. In this play, the entrance is below and in front of the first platform. The mouth or the curtain is directly under the edge of this platform. Hell itself is invisible beneath the platform. The entrance to Hell is really on the lowest of three stage levels. Hell itself is also on this level, but it is really off stage.

Only one other play definitely suggests that the entrance to Hell was placed on a lower level. In the *Aucto de la Culpa y Captividad*,[33] Culpa locates her *cueva* home as follows

> "Yo moro en este breñal   (50)
>   de serpientes
> do todos los deçendientes
>   de Adan tienen de *bajar*,"

When Cautividad later endeavors to inveigle Bobo to enter her precinct, the following dialogue occurs:

> [C.] "Baja aqui . . .
> [B.]   No bajare."   (194)

During the action of the play many characters enter Hell. Whether, before entering, they actually moved down to a lower level in full view of the audience is not entirely clear. They may simply have walked off the stage, leaving the descent to be imagined as taking place afterwards.[45]

The entrance to Hell may have been placed on a lower level much more generally and frequently than appears from the available evidence. From the indications afforded by the *Consueta del Juy* and the *Aucto de la Culpa y Captividad,* it is clear that it sometimes took such a position. The lower-level Hell-mouth in the Majorcan play may be considered a further sign of close adherence in Eastern Spain to the staging methods used north of the Pyrenees. If a similar position for Hell was used for the Castilian *Aucto,* it may indicate an extension of the system.

But several reasons might be advanced against assuming that this position for the entrance to Hell was general. In the first place,

---

[45] The text does not prove that "the cave evidently sloped downward," as Crawford inferred ("The Devil as a Dramatic Figure," 374).

no strict uniformity prevailed in France, either for the scenic representation of Hell and its entrance, or for the location of the setting. It was variously represented and was placed sometimes on the Earth level and sometimes below.[46] Indeed, as we have seen, the earliest textual record of staging in Spain, the Catalonian Assumption play of the fifteenth century, included a setting for Hell on the Earth level. In the second place, the quantitative evidence for the lower level is very slight, especially in comparison with the totality of information on the staging of Hell. The other available items are notably silent concerning the position of the entrance. Finally, the significance of this silence increases on comparison with the abundant evidence of the use of a lower level for purposes other than a setting for Hell or its entrance.

A sub-stage compartment was used to represent a dry well or pit, a well containing water, or a grave. In a performance of the *Tragedia Josephina* of Micael de Carvajal[47] Joseph was lowered into a pit and subsequently raised from it. The dialogue graphically describes the action in which the brothers tie up Joseph and lower him into the hole:

> "ru. veys aqui traygo vn cordel   (762)
>
>   . . .
>
> ne. pues no hagas ñudo ciago   (765)
>   sino vna buena lazada
>
>   . . .
>
> ga. Ora sus que hecha esta   (769)
>   tu rapaz llegate aqui
>   vosotros asi de ay
>   vosotros tened de aca
> ne. ora tumbe haziaca
>   tene muy bien de la soga
> ru. passo [passo] que se ahoga
>   vn poquito le afloxa"

[46] Stuart, "The Stage Setting of Hell and the Iconography of the Middle Ages," in *RR*, IV (1913), 330-342, especially 341-342; also the same author's *Stage Decoration in France in the Middle Ages, passim*, especially 110-111, 129 ff. Cohen, 84, still refuses to recognize a lower level Hell, visible to the audience. Chambers records several uses in early English plays of the Hell mouth placed on a lower level (*The Mediaeval Stage*, II, 137, 142).

[47] Ed. Gillet.

Joseph interrupts with a beseeching entreaty, but Zabulón cuts him off with

> "Dexate desse halago;   (789)
> tene desse cordel vos."

and, a few lines later, Gad exclaims,

> "vistes el golpe que dio   (797)
> alla dentro en el fondon"

Their elaborate activity in the subsequent raising of Joseph is no less vividly explained.

> "as. no se como le saquemos   (869)
> dan. aqui esta presto el cordel
> sy. alçale y tira del
>   que todos te ayudaremos.
> dan. Pareceme que esta muerto
>   segun pesa este rapaz
>   ysachar tu alla te haz
>   porque salga por concierto
> ju. ea ea sali a puerto
>   soñaraste reyezito
>   . . .
> as. alto alto que hazemos   (901)
>   que los mercaderes vienen

When Reuben later returns, alone and at night, to the well, he says,

> "Quiero echalle este ramal   (1193)
> y sacarle he ya de alli
> sus joseph asete ay
> ea sus alto zagal"

The well that was so necessary to the action just described must have been provided by a section of empty or unencumbered space beneath the main level of the stage, large and deep enough to conceal a man's body. Joseph was definitely lowered out of sight and later raised to the stage floor. Reuben dropped a rope into the same pit. The author would have avoided such rough realism as the text implies if he had not had the means to translate it literally into action. It seems likely that the lower compartment was reached by a simple hole or trapdoor in the stage floor.[48]

In the *Aucto de Quando Sancta Elena Hallo la Cruz de Nuestro Señor*, Judas was temporarily imprisoned in a similar pit or dry well.[49] The wells employed in the *Aucto de quando Jacob fue huyendo a las tierras de Aran* and Lope de Rueda's *Auto de los desposorios de Moisén* were supposed to contain water. The water could easily have been imaginary, however, without impairing the stage illusion, and the wells themselves may not have been very different from the pit of the *Tragedia Josephina*. In the first play Jacob removes the lid from the well, lowers water containers into the hole and then withdraws them presumably full of water.[50] In Rueda's *auto* Moses leans over the edge of the well and plunges a jug down into the imaginary water while a Bobo clings to his foot to prevent him from falling into the hole.[51] The lid that covered the well in the Jacob play may have been more generally used than the text of the other plays indicates. The well containing water may have been less deep and spacious than the dry pit, since it did not have to conceal anything so large as a human body. But an invisible sub-stage compartment was equally essential for both.

[48] Gillet states that for a performance, "there would be some contrivance to represent a well, into which the slender youth is thrown with a great show of brutality" (*Josephina*, lii). See also below, pp. 78-79. One could imagine semicircular walls raised a few feet at the edge of the stage or even circular walls entirely on the stage sufficiently high to permit the concealment of an actor. The semicircular walls would utilize a sub-stage level as much as the trapdoor would, and either alternative would imply a more elaborate setting than would be required by the trapdoor arrangement. Furthermore the well for Joseph was conventionally represented in the other arts with such a low wall (only a few inches above the ground) or no wall at all, that only a trapdoor could have fostered the illusion of Joseph's disappearance from the spectators' sight. (Cf. Laborde, *La bible moralisée illustrée*, I, Planche 23; Holbein's *Icones Historiarum Veteris Testamenti*, fac-simile reprint of Lyons edition of 1547.

[49] Rouanet, *Colección*, II, Num. XXXIII (pp. 21 ff.) 411-414, 436-437, 438, 441-445 SD. Later in the play, the same or another pit may have concealed the three crosses and the nails which Judas so industriously seeks (513 ff.) and finds (531-547).

[50] Rouanet, *Colección*, I, Num. IV (pp. 51 ff.), 289, 291 SD-294, 299, 304-308. The same kind of well may also have been more than imaginary in the anonymous *Auto de los desposorios de Ysac* (Rouanet, *Colección*, I, Num. V (pp. 67-90), 200 SD, 204-210, 231-232, 249, 328, 369, 618, 644-645), and possibly also in another *auto* of the same title (*ibid.*, Num. VI (pp. 97-115), 252-253, 259-260, 276-277, 283, 390).

[51] *Obras*, ed. Cotarelo, II, 376-377.

Space beneath the stage floor was employed as a grave in another group of plays. Toward the close of the *Aucto de la visitaçion de Sant Antonio a Sant Pablo,*[52] St. Paul is buried in a grave dug on the stage by two lions. Stage directions indicate this action as follows: "Salen dos leones y van a besar los pies a San Pablo." (368) and "Cavan la sepoltura con las manos." (373). St. Anthony places the body in the grave with these words:

>   " Ya, Señor, ya se lo qu'es;   (374-379)
>   no ay de que tomar espanto,
>   que tu lo mandas, y quies
>   *que se entierre aqui* este santo,
>   pues, quiero hazello yo, pues.
>   Quedad, cuerpo, enorabuena,"

The stage of the *huerta de Doña Elvira* in Seville must have been equipped with a trapdoor leading to a similar grave beneath the floor. In Juan de la Cueva's *Comedia del principe tirano,* the prince buries two human bodies in a grave prepared on the stage.[53] And in the same author's *Tragedia* of like title, two men are buried alive up to their breasts.[54]

A more elaborate use of the grave appears in the second act of Cervantes' *Comedia del Çerco de Numançia.*[55] First, "Haçese rruydo debajo del tablado con un barril lleno de piedras, y disparese un coete bolador."[56] Presently, "Sale por el gueco del tablado un demonio hasta el medio cuerpo . . . " (p. 139, line 21). Later "Marquino roçia con agua negra la sepultura, y abrese" (145-26), from which "sale el cuerpo amortajado, con un rrostro de muerte" (146-5). Finally both Muerte and Marquino re-enter the grave 148-12, 17-18) at the end of the act.

The grave may have been represented here by the usual simple opening with a subterranean compartment. In all the plays where this stage device was employed, no real difference can be observed

[52] Rouanet, *Colección,* III, Num. LXXVI, 261 ff.
[53] *Comedias y Tragedias de Juan de la Cueva,* pub. by Francisco de Icaza, Madrid, 1917, II, pp. 130 (argumento), 132 (argumento), 144, 147, 148.
[54] *Ibid.,* II, pp. 253 (argumento), 261-269, especially pp. 263, 268-269.
[55] Pub. by Schevill and Bonilla, in *Obras completas,* V, Madrid, 1920, 102-203.
[56] *Ibid.,* p. 137, line 25. The noise is repeated in the same act (p. 144, line 126).

in the nature of the underground hole. Except for conceivable variations in size and occasional individual details, the pit, the well, and the grave were merely different imaginative attributes applied at will to one structural element. The same opening in the floor and the same compartment below could meet the stage requirements of all three.

The grave in the *Numancia* included, however, some interesting features which the other graves did not have. In it thunderous noises were created and from it a rocket was fired. Cervantes himself credited the invention of stage thunder to a predecessor named Navarro.[57] The earliest sixteenth century notice of this stage device that has come to light applies to the year 1578, only a few years before Cervantes' work. The Corpus Christi celebration that year in Plasencia included a play on the *Naufragio de Jonás profeta*. Among other stage devices "hubo gran conmocion y tormenta con artificio de pólvora que debajo del tablado se encendió."[58] But this stage trick was much older than Cervantes supposed and, as we have seen, dated from at least as early as the Valencian Assumption play of the fifteenth century. Cervantes' opinion may indicate, however, that it had not been widely practiced until the second half of the sixteenth century.

In the *Numancia*, the grave was for the first time, definitely associated with Hell, when an infernal demon rose out of it. For the first time in Castile it is certain that Hell was represented by an invisible compartment placed on a lower level, and that the entrance, however simple, was seen by the spectators. The two lines of development in stage craft converge in the *Numancia*. Hell had been represented as an off-stage compartment, sometimes below the stage level, particularly in the East. Even when a mansion was built to represent Hell, the interior was invisible. The entrance was

<hr />

[57] "Prólogo," 7, lines 10-11. Cf. also above, p. 48, n. 26.
[58] Sánchez-Arjona, *Anales*, 97 n. 1, and Cañete, *Josefina*, xxiv. Cf. González de Eslava's *Coloquio Séptimo* for a textual preservation of the Jonas theme in dramatic literature (ed. García Icazbalceta, 84-96). It is not clear to what extent machinery beneath the stage was employed to represent the storm. Its use to a great degree, however, would not have been inconsistent either with the textual implications or the custom of elaborate staging in sixteenth century Mexico (*ibid.*, ix-xxxvii).

represented in various ways, the most striking of which was the mouth of the Leviathan. On the other hand, a lower level had long been used as a well, a pit, or a grave. The interior was also invisible and only the entrance was revealed to the audience. As in the *Numancia,* the entrance was usually a hole in the floor of the stage. But in the *Numancia* this hole was not merely the entrance to a grave but also the entrance to Hell. The uniting of these two attributes seems to have waited for the stages of the *corrales.* The pit and Hell were to continue united in the established theaters of the late sixteenth and seventeenth centuries very much as Cervantes had combined them. Toward the end of the sixteenth century Alonso López Pinciano declared that "el demonio [ha de parecer] que sube de abaxo."[59] Throughout the seventeenth there is abundant evidence, both textual and documentary, that the *escotillón* (trapdoor) was used chiefly as an exit for the Evil one.[60]

From the available material the following conclusions may tentatively be drawn concerning the representation of Heaven and Hell and the use of levels on the sixteenth century stage.

With the possible exception of the *Representació del deuallar del infern,* Heaven was always an elevated setting on a stage level above the Earth. In Eastern Spain it was occasionally a platform and elsewhere always a canopy. On the other hand, the entrance to Hell—the only visible part of the setting—was only occasionally placed on a level lower than Earth. The lower level was often used, but chiefly as a well, pit, or grave. Not until the latter part of the sixteenth century did Hell itself come to be regularly identified with the lower level. Even then, the interior was still invisible and only the entrance formed a part of the stage decoration.

The upper-level canopy Heaven appeared as a dramatic setting far more frequently than did the entrance to Hell. Furthermore Heaven was quite an elaborate decoration and usually involved

[59] *Philosophia antigva poetica,* 523.
[60] Schack, II, 265; Buchanan, 208-209; Rennert, "The Staging of Lope de Vega's Comedies," in *RHi,* XV (1906), 479.

machinery for opening and closing. Some trapeze-like apparatus, the *araceli* or a cloud or both, was usually employed in connection with Heaven. The entrance to Hell was usually no more than an exit from the stage, represented sometimes by a mere curtain. It was an elaborate setting only when the huge mouth was used. The interior of Heaven was sometimes revealed. God the Father and a host of angels were frequently accommodated inside. The interior of Hell was never visible. When an actor passed through the entrance to Hell he left the stage; Hell itself was really off-stage, whether it was located on a lower level or not.[61]

The vertical multiple stage in Spain was usually one of two levels, Earth and Heaven. The Majorcan *Consueta del Juy* is the lone example of a three-level stage, with Hell-mouth, Earth and Heaven all placed on different horizontal planes. It alone proves that such a stage was not unknown south of the Pyrenees and suggests that other performances in Eastern Spain at least, may have utilized three levels.

---

[61] There is no proof that a representation of the tortures of Hell was even attempted, as Crawford supposed ("The Devil as a Dramatic Figure," 375-376). In Gil Vicente's *Barca da Gloria*, the oars were not used as instruments of torture but as symbols of our afflictions (*Obras*, III, pp. 86 SD, 108 SD).

CHAPTER III

THE HORIZONTAL MULTIPLE STAGE IN THE SIXTEENTH CENTURY

A few documentary notices and about two score dramatic texts indicate the continuance of the horizontal multiple stage in the sixteenth century. The documents are rarely more than suggestive, but the texts are usually quite definite. Although many descriptive details are lacking, the lines and stage directions permit a reconstruction of the method of staging to the extent of showing clearly that performances of these plays must have used the horizontal multiple stage. It will be seen that in some instances simultaneous settings were definitely employed; in others the evidence reveals only multiplicity of locations. Sometimes one of the locations was decorated with setting or properties or both; sometimes no stage decoration whatever is indicated. For all these plays, however, —complicated or simple, elaborately or poorly decorated, with settings or without them—some form of multiple stage provided the means of performance.

Notices of staging are not wanting in the sixteenth century, and indications of elaborate scenery and properties are plentiful. But only occasionally do these indications show that the multiple system was followed in the arrangement of the stage. The famous edict of Charles V in 1534 "prueba cumplidamente que no era tan pobre el aparato escénico de los teatros de esta época como acaso se piensa."[1] The phrase, "con mucho aparato" was frequently applied to performances given in different places and under various circumstances as a summary description of the material aspects of the staging.[2] Perhaps such a characterization would apply to cer-

---

[1]Schack, I, 324.

[2] E.g., in the palace at Aranjuez in 1548, according to Calvete de Estrella (Pellicer, *Tratado histórico*, 31), in the market place at Toro in 1552 (Fernández Duro, "Apuntes," 234c; Cotarelo y Mori, *Obras de Lope de Rueda*, I, xiv), and the public performance of an anonymous *Representación de la Paz y Amor* at Plasencia in 1562 (Cañete, *Josefina*, lxxii).

tain stage devices like the large and realistic oven used at Plasencia in 1563 for the *Tragedia de Nabuc Donosor* or the expensive
tramoyas made for the Corpus *autos* of Seville four years earlier.[3]
But none of these notices provides the slightest information on the
method of staging.

A few available items do suggest, however, that a multiple stage
was sometimes in force. For the *Representación de las tres Marías,*
performed inside the churches of Gerona and Majorca in the sixteenth century,[4] a scaffold was erected before the high altar. On
the scaffold appeared three persons, who represented Jesus, Mary
and Joseph. In another part of the church—at the main portal or
at the doorway of the sacristy—three young priests who played
the title rôles began to sing. From this position they moved to the
scaffold to adore the Holy Family. At the same time another group
of singers appeared at the choir entrance, took part in the pro-
ceedings and again withdrew inside. Thus three sections of the
church were used, and at least one of them was equipped with
special setting—the scaffold. The choir entrance and the scaffold
were probably parts of the same location, for after the three priests
reached the platform they communicated at length and quite naturally with the singers of the choir.[5] But the main doorway or the
entrance to the sacristy probably represented a different place of
action. As the characters moved from this position to the scaffold,
they seem to have been passing from one location to another on
the large multiple stage provided by the nave or transept of the
church. This performance resembles, in part, that of the fifteenth
century Assumption plays at Valencia and Elche, where large por-
tions of the church were used for the pilgrimage of the Virgin or
for the approach of large groups of characters.

Simultaneous settings may also be inferred for two other per-

[3] Sánchez-Arjona, *Anales,* 16, 18.
[4] For a full description of this dramatic ceremony, see *España sagrada,* XLV,
20; J. Villanueva *Viaje literario,* XII, 204-205, 342-343; Schack, I, 330 n. 1; Milá,
Obras, VI, 211.
[5] Villanueva, XXII, 194. The *unguentarius* of Prague versions of the Three Mary's
play (Chambers, *Mediaeval Stage,* II, 33) seems not to have entered the liturgical
ceremony in Spain.

formances in Majorca—one a play dealing with Mary Magdalene, the other an Easter play. For the former three sections of the church were again used, the *consueta lemosina* of the sixteenth century reading: "E quant vindra en aquell pas que la Maria aura á cantar dels cossos resucitar seran aparellats davall laltar major set ó vuyt fedrins, ó tants quants volran, ab camis, é cuberts los caps ab amits; e quant vindra lo loch de resucitar, axiran davall laltar é radolant fins baix al darrer graho, anarsen an á la sacristia." The *Consueta* gives further details concerning an angel who was to sing "desde encima de la capilla de San Gabriel."[6] Perhaps the sacristy entrance merely served as an exit from the position before the high altar. But the chapel of St. Gabriel seems to have been an additional and quite separate location since there was apparently no communication between the "fedrins" and the angel. It is uncertain what places were represented by the altar and the chapel, although the former may have been imagined as a tomb as in the liturgical drama at Sens.[7] Of the Easter play mentioned above, Llabrés says, "el copista declara al principio de la obra que aparecen en ella veinte personas, hecho que acusa una tendencia a la mayor tramoya y aparato escénico, ya notado en otras, en las cuales se declara que hay que levantar *dos catafalcos o tablados*, ..."[8] These two platforms very likely constituted settings for the different places of action, as platforms had similarly done in Majorca in the fifteenth century.[9]

A sixteenth century Christmas *"Representacion* hecha en la Santa Iglesia de Sevilla, por Pedro Ramos, notario" also seems to have employed a multiple stage. According to Alenda's summary of the play: "Reprendida la Hipocresía por la Santidad, enciérrala en una cárcel, con ayuda de la Soberbia y la Gula. Pero la Templanza y la Humildad, que llegan en hábito de romeros, derriban las

<hr />

[6] Villanueva, XXII, 195-196.
[7] "Angelus autem sublevans tapetum altaris, tanquam respiciens in sepulchrum, . . ." (DuMéril, *Les origines latines du théâtre moderne*, 99). Cf. also Neil C. Brooks, *The Sepulchre of Christ in Art and Liturgy*, 59 ff., 65; also P. Raimundo González, "El teatro religioso en la edad media," in *CD*, CXV, 184-185; also Young, *The Drama of the Medieval Church*, I, 113; II, 507-513.
[8] "Repertorio de 'Consuetas' representadas en las iglesias de Mallorca (siglos XV y XVI)," in *RABM*, V (1901), 925.
[9] Cf. above, pp. 26-27.

puertas de la cárcel, anunciando que ha nacido el Redentor del género humano, y a pesar de la resistencia de sus adversarios, se marchan cantando con la Santidad, a ver al recién nacido."[10] If we may judge by this account, separate locations were needed for the jail and for the Nativity scene. Indeed the jail may have been represented by a mansion with doors and the location for the infant Jesus perhaps with a manger and other parts of a *Nacimiento*.[11]

The clearest documentary record of the horizontal multiple stage in the sixteenth century deals with the performance at Seville in 1580 of a Jesuit school play entitled *Tragedia de San Hermenegildo*.[12] According to the contemporary manuscript account, the stage for this performance appeared as follows: "El tablado era de un estado de alto y 39 pies en cuadro; en el frontispicio había una gran puerta de muy galana architectura, que representaba a la ciudad de Sevilla, en cuyo friso estaba un tarjetón con aquestas letras: S.P.Q.H. A los dos lados de esta puerta, de una parte y otra, corría un hermoso lienzo de un muro con sus almenas, fuera del cual, como espacio de tres pies, salían dos torres algo más altas, de las cuales la que estaba a mano izquierda sirvió de cárcel a San Hermenegildo y la que esta a mano derecha de castillo de los entretenimientos.[13] *A los lados de estas dos torres quedaba suficiente campo, por donde salían todas aquellas personas que representaban estar fuera de Sevilla, como el rey Leovigildo y otros;* porque por la puerta de enmedio solamente entraban y salían los que representaban estar dentro de Sevilla, como San Hermenegildo, etc."[14]

This account suggests the possibility of simultaneous settings and specifically designates simultaneous locations. The stage decoration for the city of Seville consisted of an entrance, a wall, and two towers. These decorative elements may have formed a single setting. But if the space between any of them was foreshortened,

---

[10] "Catálogo," in *BRAE*, VIII (1921), 268-269.
[11] Cf. below, pp. 94 ff.
[12] Sánchez-Arjona thought the play was written by Juan de Malara (*Anales*, 39-42), as indeed appears likely since the latter names himself the author of such a dramatic work, if not this very one, in his *Recebimiento que hizo la Ciudad de Sevilla al Rey D. Phelipe II* (fol. 147, recto).
[13] The *entretenimiento(s)* were performed between the acts of the tragedy.
[14] García Soriano, "El teatro de colegio en España," in *BRAE*, XIV (1927), 538-539. Sánchez-Arjona has also published this passage (*Anales*, 41-42).

each of the elements so affected was an individual setting. Such a foreshortening is suggested by the phrase "como espacio de tres pies" for the distance between the wall and the towers. The wall and the towers may then have been simultaneous settings instead of the several parts of a single setting. The jail and the entrance to the city may have been considered so far apart as to represent separate places on the stage. Thus the stage decoration may in itself have constituted a multiple stage.

Such a stage is definitely indicated in the specific designation of the undecorated space beyond each tower as a separate location. While the wall between the towers represented the city, the space beyond them represented some distance outside the city. The distance between these two locations—one decorated for the city, the other undecorated for the country—was foreshortened by the reduction of several miles to a few feet. This imaginative division of the stage platform into two locations is confirmed by the text of the play itself. Stage directions for Acts I and II indicate the simultaneous presence of both the gate of Seville and Leovigildo's camp in the country outside the city.[15] No communication takes place between the two locations except as actors move from one to the other. The performance of the *Tragedia,* then, certainly utilized a multiple stage, upon which appeared simultaneous locations, at least one equipped with stage decoration; and possibly this stage decoration itself was composed of simultaneous settings.[16]

The best evidence as proof and illustration of the horizontal multiple stage in the sixteenth century is to be found in the dramatic texts. Not only did texts constitute the chief evidence for the multiple stage in the fifteenth century and for the vertical multiple

---

[15] García Soriano, 548 ff. It is to be regretted that this and the other texts in the valuable Academy of History manuscript are not being printed in their entirety. From the two plays published by González Pedroso (*BAE,* LVIII, 123-143) and the fragments appearing in García Soriano's study only a most imperfect idea can be derived of the staging methods of the school drama.

[16] In the Jesuit drama in Germany there were many "Spuren der alten, *geteilten* Mysterienbühne" (Schmidt, *Die Bühnenverhältnisse des deutschen Schuldramas und seiner volkstümlichen Ableger im sechzehnten Jahrhundert,* 157-164). Cf. also Fischel, "Art and the Theatre," in *The Burlington Magazine,* LXVI (1935), 66.

stage in the sixteenth, but the documentary evidence just presented
above for the horizontal multiple stage was intimately associated
with particular plays. Each of the above items was either originally based on dramatic texts or actually appeared in conjunction
with a text. The texts themselves offer at best only a partial indication of the staging. From them it is impossible to reconstruct a
complete picture of a performance. From a text, however, it is
nearly always possible to discover the general characteristics of
the simplest possible stage for a performance.

The fact that the evidence of the texts is incomplete and limited,
however decisive it may be in revealing general characteristics,
has been a major factor in determining the manner of its presentation in this study. In this chapter the plays will be examined in two
main groups, according to their minimum staging needs. Group I
will contain the plays that require simultaneous settings, group II
those that require simultaneous locations. A small third group consisting of a few doubtful or problematical plays will be discussed
briefly. Minor groupings within these groups will be made whenever possible. It is understood that most of the plays in group II
and some of those in group III *may* also have been performed with
simultaneous settings.

The method of staging one play was probably never exactly used
for another, even in the rare instances where the same subject or
theme was treated. Nevertheless, the analysis of a few texts will
serve to illustrate the kind of evidence the texts yield and also the
method of visualization which has been applied to all. In each group
an attempt will be made to present the detailed analysis of a representative play—not necessarily the most elaborate in staging, and
neither the most difficult nor the easiest from the standpoint of
visualization. The *Quinta Angustia* has been selected for full
analysis as the typical text in group I because both dialogue and
stage directions—and chiefly the former—are essential to a reconstruction of its performance. For the other plays in each group,
the results of analysis and visualization will be recorded as briefly
as possible and in as accurate a chronological order as is at present

possible. References will be given to significant textual passages. These will frequently be quite long, since the proof of a staging method rarely lies in the evidence of a single line but in the continuity of dramatic action revealed by a large section of the text.

I

1. *Auto de la Quinta Angustia que Nuestra Señora passo al pie de la cruz*[17]

The action of the anonymous *Auto de la Quinta Angustia* occurs in three different and widely separated places, each of which is identified by setting peculiar and applicable only to itself. The play begins with the entrance of Joseph of Arimathea (1 SD), who asks a page if he may see Pilate.[18] The page replies,

> "Sí, señor, bien puede entrar   (23)
> que agora se fue assentar
> en su tribunal y trato."

In the following verse Joseph addresses Pilate and then formulates his request for Christ's body. To make certain whether or not the body is really dead, Pilate decides to summon the centurion and says to the page,

> "Llama aca   (41)
> a Centurio; corre, ve,
>
> Page.
>
> Centurio, señor, veni,
> que Pylato hos llama alli.

[17] This one-act play of 601 verses was printed at Burgos in 1552, according to the colophon of the text published by Crawford, in *RR*, III (1912), 300. For the possible authorship of Timoneda, see Gillet, "Timoneda's (?) *Aucto de la Quinta Angustia,*" in *MLN*, XLVII (1932), 7-8. Although "there is no clue to determine the . . . place of representation" (Crawford, *ibid.*, 280), there is no doubt that the play was written to be acted and not merely recited. This is emphatically demonstrated by the stage direction that indicates the fainting of Nicodemus ("Aqui se desmaya Nicodemus," 291).

[18] Timoneda's version of this play, reprinted in *RyF*, XLVIII (1917), 489-496, by Father Olmedo from a unique copy of the 1558 *Ternario Spiritual*, is somewhat longer, containing an introductory monologue by Jeremiah and a scene between Joseph and Nicodemus before the former presents himself to Pilate.

Centurio.
                Qué manda vuestra merce?"

The centurion describes at length and in detail Christ's last moments of life on the cross, whereupon Pilate gives Joseph permission to take the body.

Joseph immediately joins Nicodemus and tells him Pilate has given his permission. Together they go on toward Calvary, carrying a sheet (*sauana*, 156) and some ointment (*vnguento*, 157). Joseph announces his intention of burying the body in a new tomb (*monumento nueuo*, 159). As they draw near Calvary they descry the Virgin, and Nicodemus points out her figure in the distance, saying,

"Veysla alli bien traspassada."   (166)

The dialogue now shifts to St. John and the Virgin Mary, who exchange expressions of their profound grief. The former suddenly catches sight of Joseph and Nicodemus and exclaims,

"Gente nueua viene aca,   (202)
señora por el camino."

Joseph and his companion soon join the mourners and proceed to take Jesus down from the cross. The dialogue for this action is, in part, as follows:

"[Sant] Juan [to Nuestra Señora]
        Desuiemonos a vn lado,   (257)
        señora, y desclauaran
        este cuerpo lastimado.

                . . .
Joseph [to Nicodemus]
        razon es que nos quitemos   (264)
        estas ropas que trahemos
        y hagamos lo que conviene,
        Echad aca la escalera.
Nicodemus.
        Está bien.
Joseph.
                Si bien está,
        poned essotra siquiera,

porque de aquesta manera,
mejor se descendira

. . .

Tomemos los encensarios   (282)
y haga, señor, como hago

. . .

Señor, enciense (h)a este lado.   (287)
Que haze? Guarde no cayga!

. . .

Dadme essa touaja aca;   (300)
tened, señor, desse cabo.

. . .

Ciñamosla por aqui   (322)
la touaja, estara bien.
Nicodemus.
Sus, dame, esse cabo a mí
y aquesotro rescebi,
y apretada ten, conten.
Joseph.
Bien apretado está, sus!
estos dos cabos echemos
por los braços de la cruz,
y sosternan nuestra luz
al tiempo que desclauemos
Juan.
Passo! No llegueys al gesto
con la escalera tan junta

. . .

Nicodemus.
Tened los pies al madero,   (337)
dadme essa tenaza aca.

. . .

Joseph.
Ay Dios! que clauo tan gruesso!   (343)

. . .

Nicodemus.
Tened y desclauare   (347)
esta mano. Ya hecho es.
Descienda y descendire
abaxo y quitemosle
el clauo qu'esta en los pies.

. . .

Maria.

> Echamelo aqui, señores (357)
> echaldo aqui en mi [s] regaços
> Hijo mio, o qué ·dolores!

Joseph then asks Our Lady's permission to carry the body (*lleuallo*, 373) to the tomb, and the Virgin herself takes Our Savior's head and Mary Magdalene his feet (375-391), the stage direction reading,

> "Aqui lo lleuan al sepulchro cantando aquel verso
> que dize. 'In exitu Israel de Egypto domus Jacob
> de populo.'" (391)

During the singing, the group reaches the tomb as St. John's invocation indicates (392 ff.). After the burial Mary insists on taking a last look into the tomb at the body of her beloved Son. She cries,

> "Dexame llegar a ver (422)
> essa angelica figura
> do le fuystes a meter,
> que sepultais mi plazer
> con él en la sepultura."

The whole party presently leaves the tomb (475, 480-481), all offering consolation to the Virgin. They return to Calvary (529-531) and bless the cross as the instrument of saving mankind (537 ff.). The play ends as they all plan to return to their homes (577 ff.).

From the action of the play, it is evident that three settings were required for a performance—a chair or bench at Pilate's court, a large cross on Calvary, and a tomb at the burial spot. The chair was necessary: first, because the page told Joseph that Pilate had just sat down in his tribunal; second, because Pilate could not have displayed such a shocking lack of dignity as to seat himself on the floor and thus appear lower than his inferiors; and third, because the representations of Pilate in the non-literary arts show him en‑ sconced in a spacious, judiciary bench.[19] The absence of a chair

---

[19] Cf. Mayer, *Geschichte der spanischen Malerei*, I, 59, Abb. 32. See also the similar rendering of Solomon in an Escorial ivory (Calvert, *The Escorial*, plate 129). See also below, pp. 74 n. 28; 101.

would have been in defiant contradiction to the explicit words of the text, to every conception of verisimilitude, and to convention itself in the representation of this scene. The use of a large cross for the deposition scene is amply proved by the vivid and detailed dialogue between Joseph and Nicodemus. The action that accompanied their words could not have taken place unless a large cross appeared on the stage. With the aid of two ladders, and provided with a large piece of cloth (*sauana*, 156; or *touaja*, 300 etc.), and a pair of pincers (*tenazas*, 338 ff.), they climbed the cross, pulled out the nails after much effort, carefully lowered the body and placed it in the care of Our Lady. The dialogue consists largely of commands, exhortations and exclamations. Such words would be accompanied by corresponding action on the stage. That the action indicated for this scene could have taken place without setting for the cross and without some of the properties indicated is utterly incomprehensible. The resultant pantomine, without the removal of a body, probably in effigy,[20] from a real cross, would have been meaningless even as burlesque, which is utterly contrary to the sober reverence of the play. Furthermore, the last scene of the play again takes place before the cross, which is invoked and praised in a series of devout, lyrical passages. The delivery of these speeches to empty space would have further impaired the gravity of the whole play. Thus the cross and the stage properties are indicated by the lines of the play, and the accompanying action required their appearance on the stage. Furthermore the painting and sculpture of the period thoroughly confirm the use of these scenic elements. Of course, in the plastic arts the cross itself is always an inevitable feature. But of all the reproductions provided by the works of Mayer, Weise,

---

[20] An image was used as a stage property or fixture to represent the Virgin in *Coplas de una doncella y un pastor* (Gallardo, *Ensayo*, I, Num. 574, cols. 710-711) and in two plays called *Auto de la Resurrecion de Christo* (Rouanet, *Colección*, II, Num. LX, 514-542, lines 545 ff.; *ibid.*, III, Num. LXI, 1-18, lines 250 ff.). In the former Rouanet believed that Mary was represented by "une image ou statue de la Vierge" and in Num. LXI by "une statue ou une peinture" (*ibid.*, IV, 295, 297). In Timoneda's *Aucto de la iglesia*, ed. Johnson, Esglesia, *pastora*, enters "ab vna artifficial Esglesia en la ma" (p. 44, line 40 SD). For further information on the use of a doll or a small image, cf. Gillet's article in *PMLA*, XLIII (1928), 617-620.

Gomez-Moreno, and Calvert, only one shows a descent scene without a ladder and the majority contain two ladders.[21] The third setting, the tomb, is likewise indicated by the lines of the dialogue and the action corresponding to them. Additional evidence, however, lies in the specific reference to *"sepulchro"* in the stage direction which explicitly indicates the burial.[22] The body must have been placed in some kind of box or case, for St. John addresses the tomb and Our Lady subsequently peers into it. Furthermore, the tomb was one of the most frequent settings in the sixteenth century, appearing as a positive element of stage decoration in at least nine other early plays.[23] In all these plays it may

[21] Cf. Calvert, *The Escorial*, Num. 228; ———, *Sculpture in Spain*, Num. 81; Gómez-Moreno, *Provincia de León* [Vol. II], Num. 366 (cf. also I, p. 270); Mayer, *Die sevillaner Malerschule, Abb.* 10; ———, *Geschichte der spanischen Malerei*, I, Abb. 26, 111; ———, *Spanische Barok-Plastik*, Num. 81; Georg Weise, *Spanische Plastik aus sieben Jahrhunderten*, I, Tafel 4; III, Tafeln 298, 400, 426.
    Gabriel Llabrés says ("Repertorio," in *RABM*, V (1901), 920-927) that in Majorca in the sixteenth century or earlier "en la ceremonia del descendimiento el día de Viernes Santo un dúo entonado en latín por dos sacerdotes representando José de Aritmatea y Nicodemus, vestidos con la túnica romana, *con martillos, tenazas, y escaleras*, llevan a cabo la ceremonia cantando el *Christi*, . . . (926), and also that "Esta ultima ceremonia se verifica aún todos los años en Benisalem, pueblo del autor" (926 n. 1). The ladders and the other properties were used in Valencia between 1517 and 1523 for the Mystery of the *Deuallament de la Creu* (cf. Corbató, 83, 152). The ladder as a scenic property was used as early as 1380, when Jacob's ladder appeared in a Valencian procession (Mérimée, *L'art dramatique*, 10).
    [22] This stage direction is one of only eight in the entire play; it is the longest and the only one which reveals any information on the settings. As in most of the sixteenth century texts, the stage directions are primarily concerned with the action of the players, and mention of settings or properties is only incidental and occasional.
    [23] These plays are: (1) Juan del Encina, *Representacion á la muy bendita pasion y muerte de nuestro Redentor* and (2) *Representacion á la santísima resurrecion de Cristo*, in *Teatro Completo*, ed. Cañete and Barbieri, pp. 29 title, 33, 43, 50, 53 *(monumento)*; 34, 38, 50 *(sepultura)*, 43, 49 *(sepulcro)*. The necessary use of the tomb was implied by Cotarelo y Mori, *Juan del Encina y los orígenes del teatro español*, 51. Kohler employed the tomb as the basis for his conclusion that the two plays were performed in the chapel of the Duke of Alba's palace, *Sieben spanische dramatische Eklogen*, 22. (3) Lucas Fernández, *Auto de la pasion*, in *Farsas y eglogas al modo y estilo pastoril y castellano*, ed. Cañete, p. 252 SD and Dialogue *(monumento)*. Cañete, "prólogo," xciii, etc., Kohler, 68, and Crawford, *Spanish Drama before Lope de Vega*, 54-55, all concur in this view. (4) Gil Vicente, *Auto da historia de Deos*, in *Obras*, ed. Mendes dos Remedios, I, p. 171 SD. A *tumba* is brought on the stage. (5) Micael de Carvajal, *Tragedia Josephina* (see below, p. 78). (6-7) Two Assumption plays (see below, pp. 82-83). (8) *Auto del descendimiento de la cruz* (see below, pp. 74-75). (9) *Aucto de la resurrecion de nuestro señor*, in Rouanet, *Colección*, IV, Num. XCV (pp. 66-104), 385-397 *(monumento)*. The *túmulo* in Francisco de las Cuebas, *Representación de Justo y Pastor* was present but not essential to the staging of the play (see below, pp. 116-118); it is described in detail by Morales, fol. 90r. The *sepoltura* in the *Numancia* of Cervantes might have been a grave beneath the stage floor rather than a tomb rising above it (see ed. Schevill and Bonilla, V, Madrid, 1920, Jornada II, p. 145, 126; 146-5; 148-12, 17, 19 SD).

have resembled the typical sarcophagus of the plastic arts, which was represented in Spain, from the fifteenth to the seventeenth centuries, as a long narrow stone box, rising about two feet from the ground, and was called *monumento, sepulcro,* or *sepultura.*[24] The dimensions in general suggest the size of an average man, much as do modern coffins.[25]

The three elements of stage decoration in the *Quinta Angustia* were simultaneous settings. However close to each other they may have been placed on the stage, they could not be considered parts of a single setting, because they represented different places of action and these places of action were imagined to be a considerable distance apart. Pilate's court was not thought of as adjacent to the hill where crucifixions regularly took place, and neither spot was supposed to be near Joseph of Arimathea's new tomb "which he had hewn out in the rock."[26] Furthermore the settings which appeared at these three places were mutually exclusive. A huge cross or a burial tomb would have appeared incongruous beside Pilate's tribunal unless they were considered as different settings. The same incongruity would have been felt in regard to any two of these three settings combined at one location. The three settings were juxtaposed, and perhaps very closely, but the distances between them were immeasurably lengthened by the imagination of the spectators.

Finally, the simultaneous appearance of these three settings and the fact that they were imagined as separate from one another is shown by two important considerations. First, the action of the play is uninterrupted and Joseph of Arimathea is on the stage constantly from the first line to the last. There was thus no opportunity for the shifting of scenery or for any changes whatever in the

[24] Cf. Mayer, *Geschichte der spanischen Malerei*, II, 47, Abb. 25; Mayer, *Die sevillaner Malerschule*, Abb. 4 and 5; Weise, *Spanische Plastik aus sieben Jahrhunderten*, II, Tafeln 114, 426 and 427 (these latter two suggest the dual location arrangement of the cross and tomb); Calvert, *Sculpture in Spain*, plates 55, 115; Valbuena, 12, Fig. 1.

[25] For the performance of the *Devallament* in Valencia (1517-1523), a man was hired "per obrir e tancar lo sepulcre" (Corbató, 152).

[26] *St. Matthew*, XXVII, 60. Cf. also *St. Mark*, XV, 46; *St. Luke*, XXIII, 53.

stage decoration. All the scenic elements must have been on view from the beginning. And second, the dialogue and stage directions specifically indicate the movement of actors between the three settings. Joseph leaves Pilate and is joined by Nicodemus outside the tribunal. The text marks three stages in their passage from this setting to the cross, for after forty lines of conversation they see the Virgin Mary in the distance, and later St. John sees them as they are approaching. The movement from the cross to the tomb is specified by the stage direction (*"lo lleuan al sepulchro"*) and the subsequent return to Calvary is indicated by the dialogue (*"tornemos,"* 484; *"ya tornamos a Caluar,"* 529).

Between and in front of these settings there seems to have been some undecorated space which was doubtless imagined as a roadway connecting the settings or merely as the intervening country. It is doubtful whether it was divided with any precision even in the imagination. A part of this neutral ground[27] near Pilate's bench seems to have served as a temporary location for the centurion in the first scene—a vague, indeterminate position outside Pilate's court. The page is sent to fetch the centurion, and the latter is not considered to be in Pilate's presence until the page returns with him. The same may be said of the position of Joseph of Arimathea himself, since he converses briefly with the page before being admitted to Pilate's presence.

The text offers no clue to determine what sort of theater was used for staging the *Quinta Angustia*. From its nature and scenic elaboration, one would like to think that the play was performed either inside or just outside a church. But the action and decoration could just as well have been presented in a large private *sala* or on a magnificent platform or scaffold erected in the public square. Indeed the seventeenth century method of using several *carros* may have been employed for this play. When this method was used, the *carros* were placed close together in a straight line or slight curve, with one side open to the audience. Trestles were sta-

---

[27] Such was the *platea* in French liturgical dramas (Cohen, 25).

tioned in front of the *carros*, connecting them and providing space for the movements of the actors. The settings appeared on the *carros* themselves and were frequently mansions which housed certain actors. Pilate may well have enjoyed such a mansion in the *Quinta Angustia* instead of the mere chair we have accorded him.[28] The cross could have appeared on a second *carro* and the tomb on a third. This method is particularly plausible because it is known that elaborate *carros* were sometimes used in the sixteenth century[29] and that they were grouped in a multiple system in the seventeenth for the *autos sacramentales*.[30] It is not unlikely then that this grouping was first used much earlier than the available documentary records suggest. For the *Quinta Angustia*, however, none of the other possible theaters can be definitely rejected.

2 *Aucto del descendimiento de la cruz*[31]

The action, the technique, and the stage decoration of the anonymous *Aucto del descendimiento* follow, with slight variations, and confirm the methods of the *Quinta Angustia*. Dramatizing the same theme the *Aucto* is a little shorter; its scenes are less developed

---

[28] In the French *Mystère de Valenciennes*, Pilate had a particular *maison*, as did also Herod. Cf. Grace Frank, "Popular Iconography," in *PMLA*, XLVI (1931), 339; Cohen, 89; Jusserand, in *An English Miscellany presented to Dr. F. J. Furnivall*, 183. Herod had a chair inside a mansion in the Portuguese *Auto do Nascimento* of Baltasar Diaz (Carolina Michaëlis, *Autos portugueses de Gil Vicente y de la escuela vicentina*, Aiiij, recto, SD; [Axij], recto, SD and verso, SD).

[29] E.g., elaborate *carros*, used at Toledo in 1555, are described in the *relación* of Sebastián de Horozco, pub. by Santiago Alvarez Gamero, "Las fiestas de Toledo en 1555," in *RHi*, XXXI (1914), 401, 406, 410-411. Santiago Alvarez Gamero was one of the many pseudonyms employed by the late Raymond Foulché-Delbosc (Isabel Foulché-Delbosc y Julio Puyol, "Bibliografía de R. Foulché-Delbosc, in *RHI*, LXXXI[1] (1933), 144, Num. 343).

[30] See Pérez Pastor, *Nuevos datos*, 1901, p. 107; also the diagram pub. by Latorre y Badillo, in *RABM*, XXVI (1912), 260.

[31] Published by Rouanet, *Colección*, IV, Num. XCIII, 29-46. The performance of a play of like title was permitted at Seville in 1532. The introductory speech of Jeremiah (1-100) may be intended to call attention to paintings on *carros*, not unlike those in Francisco de las Cuebas' *Representación de los mártires Justo y Pastor* (*RHi*, XIX (1908), 431-433), or possibly to paintings or sculptures in the church. The popularity of the descent theme is further evidenced by the fact that it is the subject of four of the forty-nine plays discovered by Llabrés which were played "en las iglesias de Mallorca" in the sixteenth century or earlier ("Repertorio," in *RABM*, V (1901), 921-922, Num. 21, 25, 41, 49). Num. 25 is written in Castilian, the others in Catalan. Num. 21 bears the following significant expanded title, "Cobles del deuallament de la Creu ques fa *cade any en la SEU de Mallorca* . . ."

and are presented in a slightly different arrangement. A long introduction by the prophet Jeremiah opens the play. A scene at the cross follows immediately. Joseph of Arimathea takes leave of the grieving women to lay his request before Pilate. Then the scene in Pilate's court, the deposition scene at the cross, the funeral procession and burial at the tomb follow in the same order as in the *Quinta Angustia*. The final return to the cross is omitted in the *Aucto del descendimiento*. In spite of these small differences, the places of action in the two plays are thus identical. Calvary was again equipped with a large cross (338-340, 361-362, 366-455, especially 391-400, 451-455), and in removing the crucified body, Joseph and Nicodemus used the same properties (ladders, pincers, and winding sheet), and possibly also a hammer (273-275, 367, 374, 394, 426-435, 511). A second location was also equipped with a tomb (531-535 SD, 536-537). Pilate again had a particular location (145 SD, 223-225, 228, 271-272, 289-290, 300 SD), which may have been equipped with a chair or bench or elaborate mansion, although setting is not strictly required by the text.

When the same method of analysis and visualization is applied to other sixteenth century dramatic texts, it is found that the performances of at least fifteen more must inevitably have been presented on a multiple stage with simultaneous settings. The results of such a procedure are herewith briefly noted for each of these plays. At least two simultaneous settings were definitely essential to a performance of every one. For several three or more settings were needed. Textual suggestions are also noted of additional settings or locations which were probable or possible but not obligatory elements in the staging.

3. *Tres Pasos de la Pasión*[32]

Two settings: *a*) court scene with chairs for the four prophets (*Argumento,* p. 954), and *b*) scene on Calvary immediately preced-

[32] This anonymous play was edited by Gillet, in *PMLA,* XLVII (1932), 949-980, from the edition of Burgos, 1520. Bonilla thought this work was not one play but

ing the deposition, requiring a large cross (210 SD). Possibly an additional location where Jesus visited his mother (160 SD), and very likely another for the *Ecce homo,* which was played by an actor ("al vivo", 180 SD) and possibly revealed suddenly ("de improviso") as in the *Auto de la Pasión* of Lucas Fernández[33] by drawing a curtain which had concealed a back-stage.

4. Esteban Martín (or Martínez), *Auto, como San Juan fue Concebido*[34]

Two settings: *a*) an altar, possibly inside a structure to represent a temple (95 SD-115, 138-140, 211-215 SD, 216-220, 237).[35] *b*) The priest Zachary's house (*posada*), equipped with a *pavellón* (230 SD, 296-300, 370, 375, 385 SD).[36] Two other locations, ap-

three (*Las bacantes,* 141 n. 1), as indeed both title and stage directions imply. The latter for the *Ecce homo* and the cross merely supplement the incomplete *argumento.* However, since the *Pasos* were printed together as a unit, present in proper chronology scenes concerning the passion, and could have been performed in a single *sala,* we must consider them as different scenes in one performance rather than as different plays. The same situation may have prevailed in the lost *Cuatro casos* [sic] *de la pasión* (1533) of Pedro Sánchez (Cañete, *Farsas y Églogas de Lucas Fernández,* lxiii n. 1).

[33] *Farsas y Églogas,* pub. by Cañete, 235 SD; cf. also Gillet, "Tres pasos," 976.

[34] Gillet, in *RR,* XVII (1926), 41-64. The play may have been performed at or near Burgos in 1528 or earlier, since Moratín lists a Burgos edition of that year (*Orígenes,* 159, Num. 38). The lines of the text (34-39) indicate that the performance probably took place in the open air and in the market place.

[35] In addition to the *Auto del sacreficio de Abraham* (see below, p. 106), an altar was built on the stage in two other plays of the period: *Aucto de la ungion de David* (Rouanet, *Colección,* I, Num. XIX, 153-155, 155 SD, 184); and *Auto del sacrificio de Jete* (*ibid.,* I, Num. XXIV, 471 ff., especially 503 SD). In Gil Vicente's *Templo d'Apolo* (*Obras,* II, Coimbra, 1912), performed at Almeirim in 1526, the altar seems to have been a very durable one (pp. 178, 179 SD). It is once called marble (p. 181). For other uses of the temple, cf. the *Auto de Sanson* (see below, pp. 83-84) and the *Auto de la entrada de Xpo en Jerusalen* (see below, p. 107). In an early seventeenth century play on Cain and Abel, an "altar de piedras" is employed (Juan Caxes, *Auto de los dos primeros hermanos,* in *RHi,* VIII (1901), 139 ff., lines 1037 SD, 105 SD).

[36] This *pavellón* could hardly have been like the *palio* used in Pedro Suárez de Robles, *Danza del Santíssimo Nacimiento* (*PMLA,* XLIII (1928), 624 ff., line 1 SD), or like such a one as was placed over the bread in the *Farsa del Sacramento del amor divino* (Rouanet, *Colección,* I, Num. VII, 116 ff., lines 30-31), nor even like the *dosel* over the altar in the *Auto del sacrificio de Jete* (Rouanet, *Colección,* I, Num. XXIV, 408 ff., lines 479-480, 485, 503 SD). It is difficult to ascertain whether it sometimes concealed persons who were in the *posada,* and thus provided a sort of back-stage, as was the case with Diego Sánchez de Badajoz's *Farsa de Santa Bárbara* (see below, p. 99), or whether it served as a canopy over what was imagined as the inside of the house, somewhat like the scene presented by Diego Sánchez's *Farsa de Abraham,* where "Sara ha de estar debajo de un pabellón, y Abraham a la puerta

parently undecorated: *a*) place for Mary and Joseph (265 SD, 269 SD). *b*) Comadre's abode (345 SD, 362-368).

5. Pere Pons and Baltasar Sança, *Misteri de la Passió*[37]

Two settings: *a*) a mansion for Pilate (168 SD) with a door (136 SD), steps (136 SD, 278 SD) and a railing or balustrade (659 SD). *b*) a cross (875 SD, 903 SD). Both are represented on a platform (126 SD, 150, 839 SD) and at the same time, since characters appear at both simultaneously and pass back and forth between them (878-895 SD, 1003 SD). Herod seems to have had a definite location (422 SD, 507 SD), which may have been decorated (cf. above, n. 28). At least two and possibly six other locations seem to be indicated off the platform (799 SD, 821 SD) for *a*) Christ and the rabbis, and *b*) the group of Jews at the beginning of the play (106 SD); later for *c*) St. John (749 SD), *d*) Our Lady (754-755, 762-765 SD), and *e*) the Veronica (828 ff). And finally there may have been a special place where Christ was tortured (392 SD, 633 SD ff.). It appears at times that the whole or a large part of the church was being used as the stage (1 SD, 10 SD, 126 SD, 827 SD).

The setting for this play was doubtless one of the most elaborate in the sixteenth century. The settings and locations listed above were used for the performance on Good Friday morning. In the afternoon was represented *La representació del deuallar del infern*, which alone required three settings, Paradise and the Hell mouth, both studied above (pp. 40, 51), and a cross (1043 SD). Probably the cross was the same setting used in the morning, and it is not

---

sentado en una silla" (*Recopilación*, II, p. 181 SD). Sara's position is later referred to as "en la tienda" (*ibid.*, p. 184 SD). The earliest record of the construction of a *pavellón* for Corpus Christi entertainment appears in the accounts of the Cathedral of Salamanca for June 8, 1501: "Item. . . . fizo un criado de Calamón, carpintero, un pabellón para lo que fizo *lucas* para Corpus Christi e llevaron por lo fazer e madera dos reales." (Cotarelo y Mori, fac-simile edition of *Farsas y Églogas por Lucas Fernández*, xxi.)

[37] Pub. by Durán i Sanpere, in *Estudis universitaris catalans*, VII (1913), 241 ff. This Catalan play was written and first performed in 1534. The performance seems to have been repeated "diverses vegades" by 1545, the year of the last recorded presentation, in the parish church of Santa María in the town of Cervera (Lérida).

unlikely that the other two settings were present from the beginning of the performances. On the following day, for a short play on the deposition (*Lo deuallament de la creu*), Pilate's mansion and the cross were again used (1227 SD, 1234-1235 SD, 1241 SD, 1271 SD), and probably also an additional setting for the tomb (1294 SD). If the stage was set for all three performances before the series began on Friday morning, at least five settings appeared simultaneously (Paradise, Pilate's mansion, the cross, the tomb, and the mouth of Hell) as well as several additional locations, one or more of which (Herod's, e.g.) may have been decorated to constitute additional settings.

6. Micael de Carvajal, *Tragedia Josephina*[38]

Three settings: *a*) a well in the desert (see above, chap. II, pp. 53-55). *b*) a tomb (1067-1073; 1072 SD). *c*) a chair or throne representing Pharaoh's palace (2911-2914). Joseph may have used Pharaoh's setting (3488-3489; 3496; 3533-3535), but there is good reason to suppose that he had at least a separate location (4127-4129). Potiphar's house, since both inside and outside were used, may have been represented by stage decoration (1158; a "terraced roof," suggested Gillet, *Josephina*, lii). Jacob probably

---

[38] Ed. Gillet. The *Tragedia* may have been performed in 1535 or earlier in the plaza "de la antigua catedral de Plasencia, en cuyos viejos muros se apoyaría el vistoso cadalso aparejado para la representación" (Cañete, *Tragedia llamada Josefina*, xxiii). It may not always have been played in the same way, for the Cañete text has a different act division and some passages of text are rearranged.

As Bonilla has already observed (*Las bacantes*, 141, and *RHi*, XXVII (1912), 424 n. 2), evidence that the *Josephina* was intended for performance outdoors before an audience on Corpus Christi day is to be found in the words of the Faraute, who speaks briefly in prose before each of the five Partes or acts (Parte I, lines 14-20. 34-35; III, 2-3 ("representantes . . . oyentes"), 22-24, 28-35; V, 1-4, 13). Faraute's reference to the indubitable hunger of the spectators between Partes III and IV (line 4) may mean that the time for the midday meal has passed. This and the reference to the prevailing hot, sunny weather seem to connect Faraute's words with the actual performance. They show remarkable foresight on the part of the author or else must have been composed, as far as these realistic details are concerned, either on the day of presentation or extemporaneously as the actor progressively took the pulse of his audience.

No such interruptions of the action took place, however, between the *Actos* or scenes into which each *Parte* is divided. The dialogue is frequently continuous between the *actos*, as for example when Acto I of Parte II ends with Zenobia's remark that she hears Potiphar coming, and Acto II begins with the latter's "Buenos días" to his wife. Cf. also Miranda's *Comedia Pródiga* and Palau's *Victoria Christi*.

had at least a location of his own, as is indicated by movements between his home and other settings (569-585, 683-686; 1293-1297; 4057, 4071-4072, 4083-4086, 4094-4099). The text gives no suggestion as to the representation of the jail. The scene between God and the merchants prior to the sale of Joseph doubtless took place on the roadway or neutral space connecting the settings (882-937).

7. Antonio Diez, *Auto de Clarindo*[39]

Two locations, each containing sufficient decoration to represent a section of a house including a window or door or both, and an interior floor level somewhat higher than the stage floor or street level.[40] One serves as Florinda's house (Jornada I, 395, 426-428, 430-431, 442, 448, 459-462, 470-474), the other as Clarisa's (Jornada II, 45-51, 56-58, 66-68, 72-73, 91-95); they could not both have been represented by a single location (Jornada I, 901 ff.; Jornada II, 337-362, 365, 366, 370, 391-393, 398).

8. Luis de Miranda, *Comedia Pródiga*[41]

The action of the peripatetic *Comedia Pródiga* occurs in ten or more places suggested by the text. Of these, the *posada* (pp. 89,

[39] Reprinted by Bonilla, in *RHi*, XXVII (1912), 455 ff., the play may possibly have been performed as early as 1535 (p. 395).

[40] Cf. my article, "Windows on the Spanish Stage in the Sixteenth Century," in *HR*, II (1934), 303-318. Clearly the window, and also the wall, the door, the balcony and almost any piece of stage setting, might upon occasion become a part of a multiple stage.

[41] The earliest recorded edition appeared in 1554 and was reprinted by José María de Alava, Seville, 1868 (Soc. bib. and.). There is some reason, however, to suppose that the play was written shortly after 1532 (Cañete, *Josefina*, xv). Moratín's facile explanation of the staging (*Orígenes*, 191) evades the issues and is no solution at all of the problem (cf. above, p. 6 n. 28). The play was intended for a popular performance (Mérimée, *L'art dramatique*, 307), where the greatest possible realism would be exacted. Furthermore, the performance probably took place in the city of Plasencia, one of Spain's liveliest dramatic centers in the sixteenth century.
  The action was doubtless continuous, without breaks in the performance, the division into seven *actos* corresponding vaguely to scene divisions, without reference to stage decoration or breaks in the action (cf. above, *Tragedia Josephina*, p. 78 n. 38). Breaks between the *actos* from II to V are impossible because there is no change of place and a pause in the action would violate the continuity required by the lines. Between the other *actos* there is a change in time, but this is adequately explained on each occasion in the dialogue. All the numerous changes of place occur within a given *acto*, and never between the *actos*.

96-97) and the hermitage (pp. 88, 114) may have been off stage, and the fountain (68) imaginary.[42] Settings were required for *a*) the home of Cadan: an elevated tower (p. 117)[43] and a ground floor compartment below (p. 34); *b*) the inn *(venta)* and the mansion for *Madre,* probably one setting, since the same scenery and properties were used: a table and a few chairs (pp. 39-40, 47) before a doorway *(portal* p. 41); *c*) the jewelry shop: a mansion which involved a barrier of some kind between jeweler and customers and from which were passed objects of jewelry including some gold chains (pp. 44-45)[44]; *d*) the jail: an elevated window and probably a ground-floor door with grating (pp. 60, 62, 63-64, 67); *e*) Alcanda's house; an upper-story window, reached by a ladder, and a ground floor compartment called a *corredor* (pp. 74, 90-91, 99-101). An additional location, possibly decorated, is indicated for Briana's house (pp. 82, 93, 95, 101-104). Since the settings seem to have been very much alike, the same one may have been used for several different places. The simultaneous presence of two settings for the inn and the jewelry shop is clear, however (pp. 44-45), and also the simultaneous

[42] A fountain is similarly suggested in Torres Naharro's *Diálogo del Nascimiento* when Patrispano remarks, "Y al pie desta fuente me debo acostar" *(Propaladia,* II, p. 353). Chambers accepted the same kind of evidence in *Gammer Gurton's Needle* and *Jack Juggler* as definite indication of stage scenery to represent a post *(The Elizabethan Stage,* III, 27). See below, p. 85 n. 61, for uses of a fountain.

[43] Additional illustrations of the use of the tower as a scenic element are the following: *a*) *Tragedia de los amores de Eneas y de la Reyna Dido* (ed. Gillet and Williams, in *PMLA,* XLVI (1931), 353-431), Jornada V, where some piece of structural scenery to which Dido climbed represented the tower (lines 2450-2460, 2485-2487, 2500-2501). *b*) Alonso de la Vega, *Comedia de la Duquesa de la Rosa (Tres comedias,* pub. by Menéndez y Pelayo, Dresden, 1905), pp. 98, 100, 101, 104, 105. The tower evidently contained a window (105 SD) and the Duquesa does not seem to have been "lamentándose desde las almenas" as Menéndez y Pelayo suggested *(ibid.,* xxix). *c*) *Auto del martyrio de Sancta Bárbara* (Rouanet, *Colección,* II, Num. XXXVII, 57-60, 71-73, 78-80, 106-110, 116-117, 155-156). The tower here was built on the stage during the action of the play; it contained three windows; and the building formed an integral part of the play as in the case of the *altar* (see above, p. 76 and n. 35). *d*) Lupercio Leonardo de Argensola's *Alejandra* (López de Sedano, *Parnaso español,* VI, Madrid, 1772), Jornada III, especially pp. 505-06, 514 SD, 518, 520. *e*) Fernán González de Eslava, *Coloquio quinto, de los siete fuertes* (see below, p. 85).
The tower mentioned in Timoneda's *Comedia llamada "Floriana" (Obras,* I, Valencia, 1911, p. 493) was probably spoken scenery.

[44] Agustín de Rojas confirms the use of jewelry, particularly *cadenas de oro,* on the sixteenth century stage *(Loa de la Comedia,* in Cotarelo, *Entremeses,* I, 20 *(NBAE,* XVIII), p. 348b.

appearance of Alcanda's house and Briana's location (pp. 85-86, 88-89, 101). Similar simultaneity is definitely suggested, but not at all certain, for the inn and the jail (pp. 58-59) and also for Cadan's home and the inn (pp. 35-38). At least two settings then, and possibly several more, appeared simultaneously on the stage for the *Comedia Pródiga*.

A method similar to that used for the *Mystère de Sainte Apolline* would have been admirably suited to this play.[45] Its semicircular double tier of stalls at the back of the stage would have provided as many settings as were necessary, with upper and lower story sections wherever needed. Curtains, or some other non-transparent barrier, could have been added for the jail and for Alcanda's second floor, and table and chairs for the *venta*. This method might have eliminated the "off stage" and readily created mansions for the hermitage and the *posada*. This type of stage has also the concentration of space characteristic of the later single-set stages of the *corrales* and none of the widely scattered elements of a stage like that used for the Valenciennes *Mystère*.[46] Another possible and quite simple solution of the staging problem would have been afforded by a double back-stage[47] of two floors.

Three Assumption *Autos*

Three texts present the Assumption theme,[48] and their performances apparently used the same kind of multiple stage. A few important differences in details, however, must be noted. The first *auto* does not strictly require a multiple stage, as the text now stands. But this text may not represent a complete performance. In the first place, its 179 verses mark it as one of the shortest

[45] For a picture of this setting, see the title page by Jehan Fouquet in Bapst, *Essai sur l'histoire du théâtre*, 33; also in Mantzius, II, 65; and Cohen, 86. For a succinct description, see Fischel, 54.
[46] See Mantzius, 69; Cohen, 70.
[47] Cf. the illustrations of German school plays published by Schmidt, *Die Bühnenverhältnisse*, 189-193.
[48] In view of the great popularity of this theme in Spain during both the fifteenth and the sixteenth centuries, it is strange that there is so little evidence of early Latin drama in the liturgy of the Assumption (see Young, *The Drama of the Medieval Church*, II, 255-257, 397).

plays in existence and the shortest *auto* in the entire Rouanet collection. In the second place, it deals with only the first half of the Assumption theme. The text breaks off before the Virgin is buried, and her body never rises to Heaven on the *araceli,* although a setting for Heaven is indicated (see above, p. 42). And finally, the action corresponds closely to that of the first part (140 verses) of the complete second *auto.* The short text should evidently be considered incomplete. Its fragmentary existence might be explained by an early division of the manuscript into two sections for the two different parts of the play, perhaps still performed on different days.

The second *auto* preserves a textual record of a complete performance, divided in the middle by the comic interlude of the Jews. This division may be a surviving effect of the fifteenth century two-day performances. The third *auto,* however, lacks this episode, forms a more closely knit unit, and maintains a sober and reverent tone throughout. By combining the ascent of the Virgin's spirit and that of her body, this *auto* has achieved a concentration, a dramatic synthesis of the Assumption theme, wanting in all the other extant texts.

9. *Aucto de la Asunción de Nuestra Señora*[49]

One setting for the Virgin Mary, including a bed (10, 136 SD, 178 SD).[50] Probably an additional location for the first appearance of the apostles (85-88, 93-94, 109-114).

10. *Aucto de la Asunción de Nuestra Señora*[51]

Two settings: *a*) Virgin's setting, including a bed (162-163, 186 SD, 199). *b*) a tomb (171 SD, 211 SD). Probably also a location for the first appearance of the apostles (107-131).

[49] Rouanet, *Colección,* II, Num. XXXI, 1-7.
[50] The bed is an infrequent stage property. Except in the Assumption plays, we can be certain of its use in only one other sixteenth century play, the *Auto de los desposorios de Joseph* (see below, p. 84). It is, however, very likely that the staging of Gil Vicente's *Farça chamada "Auto da India"* required a *cama* (*Obras,* II, Coimbra, 1912, pp. 257, 265 (and therefore on p. 262 *casa* is probably a misprint for *cama),* 266). A bed was a possible property in Diego Sánchez de Badajoz's *Farsa de Isaac,* in *Recopilación,* II, p. 100, and in the anonymous *Aucto de Sant Francisco,* in Rouanet, *Colección,* II, Num. XXXIX, line 40.
[51] Rouanet, *Colección,* II, Num. XXXII, 8-20.

11. *Auto de la Asumption de Nuestra Señora*[52]

Two settings: a) Virgin's setting, including a bed curtained off and resembling a back-stage (127, 229, 245 SD, 303-306, 305 SD). b) a tomb (336-339, 350-355, 376-382, 384 SD's-386) with a cover (*tapa*, 414 SD-420). The lectern (*atril*, 56 SD) early used by the Virgin may have been placed at a third location where she first entered the stage and where the angel, St. John and the apostles subsequently appeared (56, 95, 191, 245 SD).

12. *Consueta de St. Jordi*[53]

Two settings: a) the dragon's[54] lair, equipped with a post or stake to which his victims are tied (pp. 60a SD, 61b SD(2) and Dialogue). b) the King's mansion (pp. 58a SD, 58b SD) in the city (p. 62b SD) raised up on a platform (p. 60a SD). Passage between these two settings was easy and frequent although the imaginary distance was considerable (pp. 57a SD and Dialogue, 58a SD, 59a SD(3), 60a SD, 61b SD, 62b SD).

13. *Auto de Sanson*[55]

Two settings: a) Samson's cave, possibly only an entrance (85 SD, 91, 98, 123, 313).[56] b) a temple with two columns (394-401, 414-

[52] Rouanet, *Colección*, III, Num. LXII, 19-33. Sánchez-Arjona (*Anales*, 30, 69-70) and Rouanet (*Colección*, IV, 390) to the contrary, it is very doubtful whether any of the three Assumption texts can properly be identified with either of the known performances of an Assumption play in Seville (1564 and 1583). Each of these performances took place on a single *carro* and the three extant *autos* required a multiple stage which could scarcely have been mounted on one *carro*.
[53] Pub. by Llabrés, in *BSAL*, 25 abril de 1889, 57-63.
[54] See above, p. 49, for a description of this monster.
[55] Rouanet, *Colección*, I, Num. XIII, 217-231. González Pedroso seems to have understood the use of scenery in this *auto*, when he says, "Las farsas del siglo siguiente [XVI] tienen harto mas encumbradas pretensiones. . . . aparecer Sanson dando vueltas á un molino, abrazar las columnas del templo y derribarlas; . . . todo á la faz del público . . ." (*BAE*, LVIII, xvi).
[56] The cave in Virués' *Tragedia de la infelice Marcela* (Juliá Martínez, *Poetas dramáticos valencianos*, I, pp. 118 (below title); 125, col. 2; 144) was clearly a mere exit. The cave mentioned in the *Aucto de la visitaçion de Sant Antonio a Sant Pablo* may have been represented with scenery (Rouanet, *Colección*, III, Num. LXXVI, lines 24, 138-139, 148, 153-154, 173), as also may be the one alluded to in Timoneda's *Farsa llamada "Floriana"* (*Obras completas*, Valencia, 1911, p. 494). Cf. also above, pp. 48-49.

416, 427, 429 SD).[57] Stage decoration representing a flour mill (*atahona*, 371-380 SD), to the arm or shaft of which Samson was tied, may have appeared on the same location as the cave. A fourth location may have supplied a place for early scenes between the Philistines and the people of Judah (96-98, 100 SD-101, 201-202, 216-217). This place may possibly have been decorated with a tree (296-298).[58] Samson's appearance with Delilah in the second half of the play (321 ff.) may have occurred at the entrance to the cave. As many as five locations, all decorated, could have been employed in staging this play.

14. *Auto de los desposorios de Joseph*[59]

Two settings, possibly two *carros*: *a*) outside or interior courtyard of Potiphar's palace, equipped with an elevated, second-story

[57] A temple was one of the two settings mounted on *carros* for the performance of Juan Caxes' early seventeenth century (1612) *Auto de los desposorios de la Virgen:* "Duermese [Joseph]. . . . Y abriéndose el otro medio carro donde ha de estar el templo, se vera una Sirena con una harpa, y la tierra vestida de flores, . . ." (*RHi*, VIII (1901), 173, line 648 SD).

[58] The dramatic texts of the century offer abundant evidence of the frequency with which some scenic property was used for a tree: *El Misterio de Adam y Eva*, ed. Serrano Cañete, p. 9 SD, begun as early as the fifteenth century and continuing in the sixteenth; *Egloga de Torino*, in *Orígenes de la novela*, II, Madrid, 1907, p. 67, col. 2 (". . . y acostado debaxo de un pino que alli hazen traer; . . ."), probably played in Italy (Crawford, *Spanish Pastoral Drama*, 58; Diego Sánchez de Badajoz, *Farsa de Santa Susaña*, in *Recopilación*, II, p. 129 title ("ha de ir la carreta hecha un verjel"), 145 SD, 147 SD, etc. (cf. also López Prudencio, *Diego Sánchez de Badajoz*, 215); ———, *Farsa de Abraham, ibid.*, II, p. 181 title (*encina*), p. 184 SD; Lope de Rueda, *Colloquio de Tymbria*, in *Obras*, ed. Cotarelo, II, p. 89, line 122 SD, etc. ("tueco del árbol"); ——— [?], *Comedia llamada discordia y cuestión de amor*, in *RABM*, VI (1902): Cupid is tied to a tree (p. 343 col. 2; 348-1—352-1), and his bow is hanging from it (349-2; 352-1); Alonso de la Vega, *Comedia llamada Tholomea*, in *Tres comedias*, ed. Menéndez y Pelayo, Scena 3a (pp. 14-18, *ramas*); and possibly others where the text is not so precise. Cf. also pp. 85 n. 61; 103, Num. 18.

[59] Rouanet, *Colección*, I, Num. XX, 331-357. This anonymous text is probably identifiable with a performance at Seville in 1575 which had the same title and contained the identical number of *figuras* in the cast of characters (Sánchez-Arjona, *Anales*, 55). But Rouanet's identification of the text (*Colección*, IV, 180-182) with a Madrid performance in 1608 of *Los Casamientos de Joseph* by Alonso Riquelme's company must be rejected, for Riquelme himself stated "que los autos sacramentales para este presente año se estan escribiendo por Lope de Vega" (Pérez Pastor, *Nuevos datos*, 1914, 38 and n. 1). There are also striking differences between the modest scenic requirements of our text and the decoration of the later play (Pérez Pastor, *Nuevos datos*, 1901, 107). However, in view of the rarity of Joseph's betrothal as a dramatic theme (Rouanet, *Colección*, IV, 182; Cañete, *Josefina*, lxv-lxx; Baron de Rothschild, *Mistère du viel testament*, III, xxvi-lxxxii; Gillet, *Josephina*, liii), and the general similarity in stage setting, the 1575 text may have served as a model for the one attributed to Lope, which was performed on two *medios carros*.

window (148-149; 204; 235 SD; 251-252; 263; 330; 385 SD; 401-402; 415 SD; 416-417; 421-424) and a number of chairs (226-235 SD; 335-336). *b*) Asseneth's bedroom, containing a bed (471-474; 524-525) and a table (526-528, 533 ff. (the eating of honey), 580).

15. *Aucto del Emperador Juveniano*[60]

Two settings: *a*) a *fuente* or bath, possibly concealed behind a thicket (*espesura*, 53-60 SD, 85, 297-299).[61] *b*) a *palacio*—inside and outside (70 SD, 81, 85 SD, 171 SD, 194-199, 207, 211-212, 316 SD—326). In addition, at least one location was required for the *fortaleça* (96-98, 104-106, 171 SD) and the hermitage (267-273, 314, 316 SD).

16. Fernán González de Eslava, *Coloquio quinto, de los siete fuertes*[62]

Three settings: *a*) an "hermosa torre" for the *fuerte de la Confirmación* p. 64, col. 1 SD; 66-1 SD). *b*) a "casa colgada como en el aire" in the *valle del Mundo Placer* (p. 66-2 SD). *c*) Some decoration, probably a mansion, for the *fuerte del Baptismo* (p. 62-2 SD). There is also decoration for the other five *fuertes*, which may have been five settings at as many different locations (p. 69-1 SD's [2]; 69-2 SD's [3]).

[60] Rouanet, *Colección*, I, Num. XXIII, 394-407. A play of this title was performed at Seville in 1577 (Sánchez-Arjona, *Anales*, 58).
[61] It is possible that the *fuente* itself could not be seen and the *espesura* may have been a set figure on the stage or a curtain behind which the emperor withdrew. See above, p. 84 n. 58, for the use of trees, etc. Of the dozen-odd plays which make imaginative use of a *fuente*, only two others can be said to have been decoratively represented: (1) Timoneda's *Aucto de la fuente de los siete sacramentos* (*BAE*, LVIII, 95-100, *passim*, especially p. 99, col. 2), performed at Valencia in 1570 (González Pedroso, *BAE*, LVIII, 95 n. 2, and Mérimée, *L'art dramatique*, 218); (2) González de Eslava, *Coloquio Diez y Seis* (see below, Num. 17). Other probable but uncertain uses of the *fuente* may be seen in Diego de Negueruela, *Farsa Ardamisa*, pub. by Rouanet in Bib. hisp., Barcelona and Madrid, 1910; two anonymous plays called *Aucto de los desposorios de Ysac* (Rouanet, *Colección*, I, Num. V and VI); and the anonymous *Farça del sacramento de la fuente* (*ibid.*, III, Num. LXXI). The case of the *Aucto del Emperador Juveniano* is the only one where *fuente* means bath. Cf. also above, p. 80, n. 42.
[62] *Coloquios espirituales y sacramentales*, ed. García Icazbalceta, 61-70. This *Coloquio* was performed "en el camino que va de la ciudad de México á las minas de Zacatecas" (p. 61).

17. Fernán González de Eslava, *Coloquio Diez y Seis, Del Bosque Divino*[63]

In addition to elaborate properties such as a "carro triunfal" (p. 235-2 SD), there seem to have been seven different settings, one for each sacrament (pp. 202-2 SD's; 203-1 SD; 210-1 SD's; 216-1 SD's; 221-1 SD; 226-2 SD; 231-2 SD; 235 SD), and possibly others.

II

A. 1. *Égloga de la Resurrección*[64]

A large group of sixteenth century plays required simultaneous locations for their performance. These plays may all have used simultaneous settings, but from the requirements imposed by the texts, only simultaneous locations can definitely be determined. The plays differ so much from each other that no single text could be wholly considered an exact type for the entire group. An analysis of the anonymous *Égloga de la Resurrección*, however, will serve to illustrate several different staging features found among all of them. Furthermore, this text, neither the most nor the least elaborate and complicated, reveals more of these different features than any other single text. First, the play employed three simultaneous locations; second, one of these locations was provided with stage decoration; third, the other two locations are demonstrable both in connection with and entirely independent of this setting.

The *Égloga* opens with a scene in Limbo where the patriarchs are consoling each other with their respective prophecies of the Resurrection. Mary's prayer follows. Then Jesus and his angels appear. Gabriel is sent to give Mary the good news, and Jesus himself goes over to *infierno*, causes Lucifer to flee, and liberates all the patriarchs and prophets, whom he then leads over to Mary. Several of them implore her pardon, she blesses the whole group, and the play ends with a benediction sung by David.

[63] *Ibid.*, 195-238. This *Coloquio* was probably performed in 1578 (pp. 308-309).
[64] Ed. Gillet, in *PMLA*, XLVII (1932), 949-980.

Three separate locations were needed in this performance—one called Limbo for the patriarchs and prophets, another for the Virgin Mary, and a third for Jesus. Limbo may really have been considered off stage. But it was represented decoratively by gates or doors, before which Lucifer's chair was placed. The *argumento* informs the audience that ". . . vereys como los patriarchas y profetas todos puestos dentro delimbo, . . ." and that inside they will sing their prophecies all together "en canto de horgano." David refers to his location as "oscuro abismo" (6), as does Jesus when he announces to Lucifer his intention of freeing all the souls therein imprisoned (207); and Adam later tells Christ he has come from "oscuras sombras" (271). For Christ's journey to Limbo, the *argumento* reads: "Cristo llega alos infiernos (1) alas puertas delos quales halla sentado a lucifer en su infernal silla y espantado pregunta quien es y a que viene . . . Mas al fin confundido huye alos *infiernos* y Cristo llega y dize Atolite portas principes vestras, etcetera. y libra todos los patriarchas y prophetas." (p. 963). The stage directions for the same action repeat in substance the information of the *argumento*: ". . . llega cristo al infierno[65] y alla a lucifer sentado en su silla infernal . . ." (190 SD); and "Aqui huye lucifer y dize cristo atollite portas[66] y despues saca los patriarchas y profetas . . ." (230 SD). Thus Lucifer's chair and the gates of Limbo are explicitly required. The probability that Limbo itself was off stage may be inferred. And the manner of singing "en canto de horgano" would suggest that Limbo was placed in the choir of the church.[67] Each prophet could have

---

[65] The words *infierno* and *infiernos* represent merely a synecdochic attribution of Hell to Limbo, for they refer to the location of the Holy Fathers. Covarrubias explains, ". . . llamamos limbo aquella *parte del infierno* que retuuo en si los santos Padres antes de la redencion del linage humano. . . . porque respeto del lugar de los dañados *el limbo está más cercano a la superficie de la tierra.*" (*Tesoro de la lengua.*)

[66] For ceremonies practised throughout medieval and modern Europe in connection with singing the *atollite portas*, see N. C. Brooks, "The 'Sepulchrum Christi,'" in *JEGP*, XXVII (1928), 147-161. Cf. also Chambers, *Mediaeval Stage*, II, 4-5.

[67] If the play was performed in front of the church, Limbo might have been placed beyond the main portal, inside the church itself and off stage.

The suggested use of the choir for Limbo, however, is amply supported by parallel examples. It occurred in Majorca in the early sixteenth century for the "representaciones de las tres Marías" (Villanueva, *Viaje literario*, XXII, 194). The Easter Play

stepped to the grating or gates of the choir when he spoke his lines. Except on these brief and infrequent occasions, the singers in the choir, whom we may presume played the parts of the patriarchs and prophets, need not have been seen by the spectators. They do not act, they rehearse no real dialogue, and each announces his own identity.

The other two locations for Mary and Jesus respectively were definitely separate and distinct from Limbo and from each other. They were necessarily different from Limbo because all three were used simultaneously, because neither Mary nor Jesus was imagined to be in Limbo or near it, and because the stage decoration of Limbo helped to keep its location constantly established before the spectator's eyes. The location for Mary was separate from that of her Son because they appeared simultaneously, and because neither conversation nor the least sign of recognition passed between them. Finally, both the simultaneity and the separateness of the three locations is indicated by the passing of actors from one to another. Such movements involving all three locations are succinctly expressed both by a part of the detailed *argumento* and by the stage directions. The former says, "Y acabada la oracion [de Nuestra Señora] el christo aparesce resuscitado con su gloria: y en compania de sus angeles y luego manda al arcangel Gabriel que denuncie esta resurection a su madre y *vase el archangel gabriel y dize a nuestra señora*. Regina celi letare etcetera y *entre tanto* que la acaban los cantores *Cristo* llega alos infiernos . . . " (p. 963). And the stage direction confirms the *argumento* as follows: "Aqui paresce cristo resuscitado . . . Aqui dize el angel a nuestra señora regina celi. y entre tanto que la cantan los cantores *llega cristo al infierno . . .*" (190 SD).

---

of Juan de Pedraza (ed. Gillet, in *RHi*, LXXXI¹ (1933), 550-607) was probably performed in church (Gillet, *ibid.*, 3) and also used the choir for Limbo (160 SD, 180 SD ff., 240, 287 SD). Gil Vicente's *Auto da historia de Deos* closely resembles the *Égloga de la Resurrección* in theme and dramatic structure and shows a similar use of the choir for Limbo (*Obras*, I, pp. 156 SD, 157 SD, 165 SD, 172 SD; cf. also Oscar de Pratt, *Gil Vicente, notas e comentarios*, 42), as does also Bartolomé Palau's *Victoria Christi* (Barcelona ed., 1670, p. 10 verso, cols. 1 and 2; 15 v., 2; 31 r., 2; 36 v., 2). Diego Sánchez de Badajoz also employed the choir as a hidden off-stage section in his *Farsa del juego de cañas* (*Recopilación*, II, pp. 267 ff.).

Thus it is evident: first that Gabriel had to move from where he and Jesus appeared to the place where Mary was stationed; and second, that, while His message was being thus transmitted, Jesus also had to move to another, a third location—Limbo. A final shift was made by Jesus and the redeemed souls when they went from Limbo to Mary's location. The argumento reads: "Y va [Jesus] a consolar a nuestra señora . . ." (p. 963). And stage directions for the respective arrivals of Adam and Eve further corroborate the need for the actual movement from Limbo to Mary's location ("Aqui llega . . .": 270 SD, 280 SD).

Two important characteristics of the staging of the *Égloga de la Resurrección*[68] appear also in a small group of five or more sixteenth century plays. These plays similarly require 1) a stage with two or more simultaneous locations and 2) a chair or chairs as decoration for one of the locations. The results of the analysis and visualization of these plays follows in a brief and summary record. For the first five texts (2-6) (both features of the staging are entirely clear.[69] For the others (7-10) there is some doubt, since the imaginary distance between the two possible locations is an unknown quantity and it is therefore uncertain whether any foreshortening of space was necessary in the performances. Nor is the stage decoration in some of these plays always a certainty.

[68] Gil Vicente's *Auto da historia de Deos* is identical to this *Égloga* in employing a location for Limbo (cf. above, pp. 71 n. 23, 87 n. 67), with a chair for Lucifer placed in front of it (*Obras*, I, p. 146 SD), and another quite separate location for Jesus (*ibid.*, pp. 168-169 Dialogue and SD's).

[69] Five Portuguese plays also used two locations with a chair or chairs placed at one of them. These plays are (1) Gil Vicente's *Farça de Ines Pereira*, which required a street (*Obras*, II, pp. 324, 325 SD, 330-331 Dialogue and SD) and inside the home of Ines and her mother (pp. 318 SD, 325 SD, 330-331 Dialogue and SD), where there were doubtless chairs (p. 325 Dialogue and SD.); (2) the same author's *Amadis de Gaula*, for which the locations were the court of King Lisuarte, doubtless containing chairs (*Obras*, III, pp. 206 SD, 208 SD and Dialogue, 211 SD), and an orchard, which may have contained a pool ("tanque," p. 208 SD and Dialogue); (3) Afonso Alvares, *Auto de Santo Antonio* (Carolina Michaëlis, *Autos portugueses*), requiring a road (Aiij, recto, Dialogue and SD—Aiiij, recto) and Conego's house, equipped with chairs (Aiij, recto, SD; [Aviij], recto); (4) the same writer's *Auto de Santiago*, which used a road (*ibid.*, beginning—[Avij], recto) and a location for Our Lady, who was probably seated ([Avij], recto, SD's); and (5) the anonymous *Auto de Dom Andre*, for which there were separate locations for a road (*ibid.*, Aiiij, verso, SD) and a house, the latter certainly containing chairs (Av, recto, Dialogue and SD).

They are listed, therefore, only provisionally, as possible or probable representatives of the multiple stage technique in a form which seems very simple and approximates a single-location stage.

2. Bartolomé Palau, *Farsa llamada custodia del hombre*[70]

In Jornada V, two locations for the *mesón de gracia* and Christ's tribunal, since Honbre's passage from one to the other may clearly be traced (4226-4227, 4240, 4262-4269; 4300-4305, 4413 SD). The second is equipped with a bench or chairs for Christ, Mercy, Justice and Mary (4484-4487, 4936 SD). In the preceding Jornada, although there exists no clue to the setting, at least two locations were employed in the similar passage from the *mesón de Iglesia* to the *mesón de Penitencia* (3867-3872, 3877-3882, 3927-3930, 3934), besides the much-used roadway. In the absence of

---

[70] Pub. by Léo Rouanet, Paris, 1911. The editor dates the play between 1540 and 1547 (p. 6). I would plead a revision of the opinion advanced by the editor that "no fué compuesta para ser representada, sino leída" and based on the presence of verses at the end entitled "El autor al lector" (pp. 6-7, 161). These verses could well have been an addition, written and prepared especially for the edition, a custom practised by some contemporary dramatists (e.g., Timoneda, for Lope de Rueda's, for Alonso de la Vega's and for his own plays). In the *Introito y argumento*, Palau addresses the spectators, asks them to listen to what "aqui se recitaran," and tells them they ought to be as desirous to see his play as they are to "ver y oyr" love farces (line 1 ff.). Later he seems to refer to a particular audience and possibly to a patroness (853-856). Clues to Palau's own intentions regarding his plays (cf. Morel-Fatio, in *BHi*, II, 238-239 and 239 n. 1) are to be found in the text of his *Victoria Christi*. In the dedication Palau says of his work, ". . . he compuesto esta obrezilla, intitulada Victoria Christi, apropriada para la Pascua de Resurrecció de Iesu Christo nuestro Redentor. Cuya materia, y principal intento es vna allegorica *representacion* del cautiverio . . ." (ed. Barcelona, 1670, p. 2). At the beginning of Parte III, Auto 5º, in an explanation of the purpose of the *Auto*, the author says, in part, "es para algun regozijo *a los oyentes, o lectores,* . . ." (p. 19). He also headed his prologue with the following title: "Prologo, y argumento general, dondequiera que se *representare* la presente obra" (p. 3). These terms leave no doubt that Palau intended his work to be played.

Now the *Victoria Christi* has a prose *prólogo* of dedication directed to the Archbishop of Zaragoza as the earlier *Custodia* had one offering the play to the Archbishop's "procurador y vicario general" (p. 12). It also has one stanza which follows the text, the "Fin" and the "Soli Deo honor, & gloria, Amen" and headed "El Autor" (p. 37), all of which corresponds to the three stanzas of the *Custodia* which follow the text, the "Fin," and the "Soli Deo laus, honor et gloria," and headed "El autor al lector." Palau evidently indulged the practice of appending a few words to his public, for the last five lines of his *Historia de la gloriosa Santa Orosia* are obviously directed to the audience (pub. by Fernández-Guerra, Madrid, 1883, lines 2360 ff.), and the same is true of the termination of the *Farsa llamada Salamantina* (*BHi*, II (1900), 304). Apparently Palau never composed a play to be read only. When the interests of readers were considered, this consideration seems to have been additional or supplementary to the play itself, and a feature peculiar to the printed plays in general.

setting, it might be objected that the travelers depart from and return to the same location, leaving the change of identity to the imagination. However, the situation is analogous to that in Jornada V where two locations were necessary. Furthermore in Jornada IV itself, at one point two different groups of personages are on stage simultaneously and not aware of each other's existence (3558-3605). If no location had to do double duty, the play could have been performed on a seven-location stage (one each for the *mesón de Luxuria*, the *mesón de Avaricia* and the *cueva*, as well as the four mentioned above, including also the roadway and an unnamed exit. Stage decoration is indicated only for the tribunal, however. All the other locations might have been little more than simple exits—passageways through curtains, openings in partitions, or positions on the edge of the stage limits. They might, on the other hand, have been mansions, elaborately constructed and decorated in the Old French manner,[71] or they might well have been represented by something between the two extremes.

3. Juan Rodrigo Alonso de Pedraza, *Comedia de Sancta Susaña*[72]

Two locations: *a*) a garden (104 SD, 117, 121-124, 187-193, 199 SD-215 SD) and *b*) a court of judgment, furnished with chairs (438 SD, 447-449, 767-774). One shift of location is indicated—from the garden to where Susaña's husband Joachim appeared (383-384), possibly in the roadway or open space between the two locations. Whether any stage property represented the *baño* in the garden is uncertain, but the branches and foliage (187-193, 199 SD, 215 SD) may very well have appeared dec-

---

[71] Cohen, 69 ff., and Planches I and III. Another 'Judgment' play was performed in Majorca with three settings on different levels (cf. above, the *Consueta del Juy*, pp. 40-41, 51-52).
[72] Reprinted from an edition of 1533 by Bonilla, in *RHi*, XXVII (1912), 423 ff. As Bonilla pointed out (424 nn. 1 and 2), the text indicates that the play was probably performed outdoors in or near Segovia (title and lines 24, 60). A performance probably occurred at least as early as 1551 since an edition of that year was recorded by Moratín (*Orígenes*, 179).

oratively, as in Diego Sánchez's *Farsa*.[73] Since no use is made of the jail, one may doubt whether it was represented on the stage at all.[74]

4. *Auto de la Degollación de Sant Juan Baptista*[75]

Two locations: *a*) a banquet scene, equipped with chairs (175 SD-185) and probably a table;[76] and *b*) a jail, to which Alguazil and Baruquel go (236-240 SD) and from which they later return to the King's banquet with John the Baptist's head (269-271).[77] The text vaguely suggests at times a more elaborate staging, with locations or mansions for Herodias, the King, and others (175, 180, 280, 283, 325).[78]

[73] The likelihood that Alonso de Pedraza's play was performed is increased by the fact that three other dramatic pieces on the same theme were performed at different places and under different circumstances during the century. (1) Diego Sánchez de Badajoz's *Farsa de Santa Susaña*, in *Recopilación*, II, pp. 129 ff., was played at a Corpus Christi celebration (López Prudencio, *Diego Sánchez de Badajoz*, 216-217) and on a "carreta hecha un verjel" (rubric, p. 129), probably in Badajoz or Talavera. (2) A short *entremés* on *Santa Susaña* was performed in a church at Christmas time (Alenda, "Catálogo," in *BRAE*, VI (1919), 761-764). (3) A Majorcan church was also the scene of a St. Susan play, according to Llabrés, "Repertorio," in *RABM*, V (1901), 931, Num. 16.

[74] There is no need to admit the tower, which appeared in the wood-cut on the title page (Bonilla, *Las bacantes*, 423) as any sort of attempt to represent a setting of the play. Indeed the bearing of such frontispiece decorations on the contents of the book must frequently enough be under suspicion (cf. above, p. 4).

[75] Rouanet, *Colección*, II, Num. XXXV, 49-61.

[76] Although neither specifically mentioned in the text nor necessarily required by the action, the table may be inferred from its appearance in pictorial representations of the scene (cf. Mâle, *L'art religieux de la fin du moyen âge en France*, 57-58).

[77] The human head appears also in two Portuguese plays as a stage property. In the anonymous *Auto de dom Luis dos Turcos* of 1572 or earlier (Carolina Michaëlis, *Autos portugueses*), toward the close of the play "Vem o Principe com a cabeça do pai" ([Axij], verso, SD). The device employed in Baltasar Diaz's *Auto de Santa Caterina* (*ibid.*) must have been ingenious, for near the end "Aqui degolam sancta Caterina & botara Leyte em lugar de sangre . . ." ([Axvi], recto, SD). In Juan de la Cueva's *Tragedia de los Siete Infantes de Lara* seven heads seem to have been brought to the banquet table (*Comedias y Tragedias*, Madrid, I, 1917, pp. 115 (*argumento*), 121. Cf. also Cueva's *Comedia del Degollado* (*ibid.*, p. 268; also Crawford, "A Sixteenth-Century Analogue of *Measure for Measure*," in *MLN*, XXXV (1920), 331.

[78] Obscurities and apparent inconsistencies in the text would thus be removed as they would also in two other plays of the same collection—*Aucto de quando Sancta Elena hallo la cruz de Nuestro Señor* (II, Num. XXXIII, 1-75 SD, 165 SD) and *Aucto de la Ungion de David* (I, Num. XIX, 275 SD, 375 SD).

5. Micael de Carvajal and Luis Hurtado de Toledo, *Las Cortes de la Muerte*[79]

Two locations: *a*) the road, which is not merely just outside Muerte's abode but sometimes at a considerable distance from it (Scene VIII and first part of Scene IX, for example; p. 13, col. 1; p. 14, col. 1; p. 39, col. 1); and *b*) Muerte's court, which was furnished with chairs or benches and possibly lights (p. 4, col. 2 SD; p. 9, col. 1 "candiles"), and may have been a structure (p. 4, cols. 1 SD and 2), which housed Death's retinue, probably including the musicians who played trumpets (p. 4, col. 1 SD; p. 4, col. 2 SD; p. 7, col. 2 SD; etc.). Passage from *a*) to *b*) is clearly indicated (p. 14, col. 2 SD; p. 33, col. 3).

6. *Aucto de la prisión de Sant Pedro*[80]

Two locations: *a*) Herod's position, probably decorated with a throne, and *b*) St. Peter's position before and when the centurion joins him (71-75, 81 ff., 116-120, 126-128). If St. Peter's prison was represented on stage, as seems likely, there is no doubt that the multiple stage technique was in force, and probably even simul-

[79] Pub. by Justo de Sancha (*BAE*, XXXV, 1-41). See Gillet, *Josephina*, xv-xix, for Carvajal's authorship. The play was first printed in Toledo, 1557. Schack (I, 377 n. 2) and Crawford (*Spanish Drama before Lope de Vega*, 150) to the contrary, the inordinate length of the play cannot be sustained as sufficient claim to disqualify it from performance. The *Cortes* is dwarfed by comparison with the French *mystères* (cf., for example, the 61,908 lines of the *Mystère des Actes des Apôtres*), although it is somewhat bulkier than other long Spanish texts of the period for which performance was certain or extremely likely (Carvajal's *Josephina*, 4256 lines; Luis de Miranda's *Comedia Pródiga*, c. 3000 lines; Palau's *Custodia del hombre*, 5206 lines, and his *Victoria Christi*, c. 4500 lines). After Hurtado's additions are removed, however, the total length of Carvajal's work becomes about 7400 verses. That he intended it to be performed is evident from both the expanded title and the *introito*. In the former we read, "Las Cortes de la Muerte a las quales vienen todos los estados, y por via de *representacion*, dan aviso a los vivientes y doctrina a los *oyentes*" (p. 1). The speaker of the *introito* asks for attention from an audience that is listening to a play, not reading a book, when he commands them, "oid los que estais dormidos" (p. 2 a and b) and "Sed atentos y callados." Carvajal's position as a popular dramatist was established by the successful *Tragedia Josephina*. In this play the Faraute tells the spectators between Partes (or Acts) II and III, "siempre gratamente seys largas oras con mucha atencion siempre he sido oydo" (ed. Gillet, 105, lines 14-15). The practicality of the staging methods implicit in the *Cortes de la Muerte* is equally evident when it is observed that the use of the cloud is in accord with the known uses of this scenic device in earlier and contemporary plays (see above, p. 44).

[80] Rouanet, *Colección*, II, Num. XLVII, 279-283.

taneous settings (182, 216, 227, 240 SD, 251-253, 295 SD, 320-321, 323-325, 340-341, 351 ff.).

The plays that may be provisionally classified with this group are the following:

7. *Aucto de un milagro de Sancto Andres*[81]

Two locations for inside and outside the Bishop's house (121-126, 159-161; 241-250, 386 SD). The house may have been a mansion slightly raised above the stage level (63); it was certainly furnished with chairs (240 SD).

8. *Aucto de Tobias*[82]

Two locations for inside and outside the house of Tobias (206-210 SD, 231-236). The former may have had a chair for decoration.[83]

9. *Auto del despedimiento de Christo de su madre*[84]

Two locations for the position of Our Lady and the roadway (1-45).

10. *Auto del robo de Digna*[85]

Two locations or a slightly extended single location for Jacob, to include the approach of the King and the Prince (154-168 SD).

B. 11-17. Seven Nativity Plays

The performances of a small group of Nativity plays also resembled the staging of the *Égloga de la Resurrección* in their

---

[81] *Ibid.*, I, Num. XXVIII, 468-482.

[82] *Ibid.*, I, Num. XXI, 358-376. A play of this title was performed at Seville in 1561 (Sánchez-Arjona, *Anales*, 26), and another at Madrid in 1593 (Pérez Pastor, *Nuevos datos*, 1901, p. 35). A third was presented in a Majorcan church some time during the sixteenth century (Llabrés, "Repertorio," Num. 34). Our play may be the earlier Seville production. At any rate the evident popularity of the Tobias theme increases the likelihood that our present text was performed somewhere.

[83] This is particularly true on account of his blindness. A seventeenth century painting by Pereda shows Tobias seated on a large frame and leather chair (Mayer, *Geschichte der spanischen Malerei*, II, Abb. 96, p. 195).

[84] Rouanet, *Colección*, II, Num. LIV, 403-420.

[85] *Ibid.*, I, Num. VIII. Rouanet (*ibid.*, IV, 152-153) thinks the author was Lope de Rueda, particularly on account of the prose scene with the *bobo*. Cotarelo (*Obras de Lope de Rueda*, I, xcv n. 1) holds the evidence insufficient. Both Rouanet and Sánchez-Arjona (*Anales*, 44 and n. 1) believe that our present text was that presented as a Corpus *auto* at Seville in 1570 under the title *Dina, hija de Cabob* [sic].

use of two locations and at least one setting. The setting in each
was some kind of decoration to represent a doorway. One of these
Christmas plays was the *Obra del Pecador* (Num.
11) of Bar-
tolomé Aparicio,[86] in which the locations were *a*) the place in
Bethlehem where Joseph and Mary stop for the birth of Jesus,
called a *portal* (pp. 232, 241) ; and *b*) the country side where the
shepherds meet (pp. 233 ff.). The shepherds pay no attention to the
Holy Family and apparently do not see them until they travel
to Bethlehem (p. 241 SD and Dialogue). The *portal* probably
contained a *pesebre* (p. 242 ff.)[87] and may have been a structural
mansion, for the shepherds speak of entering it (p. 241).
Similar to the *Obra del Pecador* were the performances of several other Christmas plays. In Perolopez Ranjel's *Farça del Nascimiento* (Num. 12) there was a special location for the shepherds
in addition to the decoration for "*a Nacimiento* set up in the
church."[88] Timoneda's *Aucto* (Num. 13)[89] also made use of set-

[86] Pub. by Gallardo, *Ensayo*, I, 221-245 (Num. 216). The play is dated about the
middle of the century (Crawford, *Spanish Drama before Lope de Vega*, 139), and may
have been performed in a church, as were Gil Vicente's Nativity play called *Auto
dos Quatro Tempos* ("na capella de San Miguel," *Obras*, III, 65), and three Christmas
autos of Jorge de Montemayor (cf. Florence Whyte, "Tres autos," in *PMLA*, XLIII
(1928), 958). The rough shepherd scene would have taken place in one of the aisles
or transepts, or possibly in front of the choir, and the location for the birth and
adoration scenes would have been more central, perhaps in the crossing or on the
steps of the chancel.
[87] The cradle was employed as a property in five of Gil Vicente's plays: *Auto
Pastoril Castelhano* (*Obras*, III, Coimbra, 1914, pp. 21 SD, 22 SD), and doubtless
the *Auto dos Reis Magos* (*Obras*, III, pp. 27 ff.), since it was apparently played under
the same conditions as *Auto dos Quatro Tempos* (*Obras*, III,
pp. 68 SD, 82 SD); *O Juiz da Beira* (*Obras*, II, Coimbra, 1912, p. 353— probably a real
cattle manger); *Auto da Mofina Mendes* (*Obras*, I, Coimbra, 1907, p. 19 SD—probably a real cradle). The *Danza del Santíssimo Nacimiento* of Pedro Suárez de Robles
(ed. Gillet, in *PMLA*, XLIII (1928), 614-634) used a "cuna al modo de pesebre"
(p. 624 SD; cf. also Moratín, *Orígenes*, 202-204), which Schack said was on the
"gradas del altar mayor" (I, 381); and something similar seems to have been adopted
by the anonymous *Aucto de la Circuncision de Nuestro Señor* (Rouanet, *Colección*,
II, Num. LI (pp. 356-373), 73-75, 79-80). Among the inanimate representations of
the manger scene, one might include Gil Vicente's *Auto de la Sibila Casandra*
(ed. Alvaro Giráldez, Madrid, 1921, pp. 37 SD, 39 SD; see also Crawford, *Spanish
Drama before Lope de Vega*, 44) along with the anonymous *Nascimiento del Hijo
de Dios Humanado* described by Alenda, "Catálogo," in *BRAE*, VI (1919), 761-
764, where the scene is portrayed on a *retablo*. The *pesebre* was evidently used in a
Nativity play at Zaragoza in 1487 (cf. Sánchez-Arjona, *Anales*, 34). For the cradle
as a traditional property in the earlier liturgical drama, see Young, "Officium Pastorum," 334-344.
[88] Gillet, who edited the play, in *PMLA*, XLI (1926), 860-890, suggests such a
Nacimiento for a performance, on the basis of boughs, a hut and a palm-tree indi-

ting for a *nacimiento*, which was concealed, probably by a curtain, until the appropriate time when the shepherds reached the doorway, as is disclosed by references in the dialogue to "vn pobre portal" (p. 225a), "baxo de su cortina" (p. 226a), "Vamos alla, quesespera," etc. (p. 226b), and by the stage direction, "Aqui se muestra el nacimiento" (p. 226b). In the Nativity play of Hernando López de Yanguas (Num. 14)[90] the shepherds move from one place to another to present their gifts to the Virgin, the stage direction reading, "Aquí llegan adonde ella está; y pide albricias Pero Pança porque la vee primero" (p. 205). And two Christmas plays written in Castilian by Gil Vicente, *Auto Pastoril Castelhano* (Num. 15) and *Auto dos Quatro Tempos* (Num. 16), both require that the shepherds move from their original location to another containing the manger.[91]

This method of performance for Christmas plays may have been quite general,[92] but the texts of other plays, like Gómez Manrique's, for example, for which claims of an elaborate multiple stage have been made,[93] do not require such a staging. Indeed the apparent simplicity of these Spanish plays on the Nativity would indicate that they may have developed quite directly from the simple liturgical drama.[94] A somewhat more elaborate staging must have survived in Majorca, however, as is shown by the text of the *Consueta de la Nit de Nadal* (Num. 17).[95] The doorway itself at Bethlehem is called a *porxo* (p. 44b) and is placed

cated in the text (282, 313, 337). Salvá seems to have sensed the multiple stage for this play (*Catálogo*, I, Num. 1298, pp. 457b; 458).

[89] Cf. Father Olmedo's reprint of a newly discovered 1558 edition, in *RyF*, XLVIII (1917), 219-227.

[90] *Egloga nuevamente trobada . . . en loor de la natividad* (Kohler, *Sieben spanische dramatische Eklogen*, 192-209), probably written before 1518.

[91] *Obras*, III, p. 21 Dialogue and SD's; p. 68 SD.

[92] Cf. Valbuena, 28.

[93] See Rodríguez, 83-87.

[94] Cf. Young, *The Drama of the Medieval Church*, II, 3-101, 400; and Parker, 180-181. Parker claims also that "the liturgical drama expanded towards the more extensive range of the Miracles, but was reduced to its former simplicity by reformatory measures" (p. 173).

[95] Pub. by Llabrés, in *BSAL*, XV (1915), 38-46. The first part of the text is missing. At the end appears the name of the author or, more likely, the copyist or *refundidor*, the place and the year: "F. R^m. P. Michaelis Pasqual, uille Buger anno 1599."

upon a *cadafal* (p. 45a SD). Characters go in and out (pp. 45a, 45b SD), and the adoration of the shepherds takes place within this mansion in full view of the spectators (p. 45b). But in addition to this setting, there seem to have been special mansions or locations for several, if not all, of the other characters. Death and Original Sin seem to have special places, for after Lucifer has directed them to guard "la porta del mon" (p. 38b), "are sen tornan La Mort y lo Original en son loch, y anantsen diu l'Original . . ." (p. 38b SD).[96] Later when Mortal Sin and Venial Sin spy Adam in the distance, they speak of jumping and running after him (p. 39a), the direction reading, "Açi salten los dos peccats" (p. 39a SD). This may mean that their places were on an elevation somewhat higher than the locality where Adam was walking. The emperor also probably had a special mansion. When the *Accusant* comes to tell him about the Sybil's prophecy, he is obliged to convince the doorman of the importance of his mission before he is permitted to enter (p. 42b). Considerable distances are imagined at times (p. 39b SD, 45a SD) and, indeed, a large part of the church must have been given over to the performance, for the shepherds enter, talk together "en mig de la sglesia" (p. 44b SD) and finally "Canten al to que uoldrán fins al cadafal de Ioseph" (p. 45a SD).

THE BACK-STAGE

In connection with these Nativity plays it is necessary to admit the possibility of a back-stage, and to determine, if possible, what effect such a device would have on the multiple stage. By back-stage is meant a recess or alcove usually at the rear of the stage, concealed from the spectators' view by a curtain. At appropriate times during the performance of a play the curtain might be drawn, and the back-stage, thus made wholly visible, became a part of the stage. The feature of the back-stage which chiefly differentiated it from any other setting or location which might form part of a multiple stage was its temporary or transient quality. It was re

96 See also a later stage direction: "Torn La Mort en son loch" (p. 42a).

vealed only when in active use and remained concealed as if non-existent when the action did not require its participation.[97] An ordinary mansion or setting—and even sometimes a location—in the simultaneous arrangement had no such means of blotting out its existence at will. The back-stage was also quite different from any recess which remained constantly off stage and invisible to the audience, as was likely in the numerous representations of Limbo.[98] The back-stage became a regular adjunct to the staging of plays in the seventeenth century *corrales*; it appeared occasionally in some form in the sixteenth century; and, if we include the entire peninsula, it seems to have provided a method for staging Nativity plays as well.

There is abundant evidence that the seventeenth century made free use of the back-stage to effect changes of scene and significant shifts of stage decoration.[99] As significant illustrations of this method three religious plays might be mentioned from the first years of the century—the anonymous *Auto sacramental nuebo de las Pruebas del Linaje Umano y Encomienda del Honbre* of the year 1605,[100] and the *Auto famoso de los desposorios de la Virgen* and the *Auto historial intitulado los trauajos de Josef, Esposo de Mª*, both by Juan Caxes.[101] It has been recognized that the plays of Caxes imitate sixteenth century themes and demonstrate a technique midway between the old and the new.[102]

In the sixteenth century only a few extant plays show the use

[97] The early English back-stage was similar (Creizenach, *Geschichte*, III, 503; Chambers, *The Elizabethan Stage*, III, 81-88).
[98] See above, pp. 86-88.
[99] Schack, II, 263-264; Buchanan, 208; Rennert, "Staging of Lope de Vega's Comedies," 460-461.
[100] Pub. by Rouanet, Paris and Madrid, 1897. The back-stage is opened no less than four times (954 SD, 999 SD, 1001 SD, 1003 SD, 1006 SD, 1039 SD; 1046 SD, 1092 SD). On the fourth occasion the stage directions show not only the elaborate tableaux with a stairway as part of the decoration but also the degree of conformity in theatrical art to the conventional conceptions manifest in the other arts ("Abrese una cortina y apareçe en un trono la Trinidad *en la forma que se pinta*, San Juan Ebanjelista en asiento de secretario, el Bautista y San Pedro á los lados, la Birgen á un lado de la Trinidad; las tres Personas mas altas que las demas" (1126). When the Demonio tries to climb up to San Pedro, "Derribale de las gradas" (1130).
[101] In the first play the curtain is opened twice, revealing a different setting each time in the back-stage (*RHi*, VIII (1901), 117, 139, lines 438 SD, 979 SD), and in the second the same stage operation occurs three times, disclosing the same scene, but with slight variations in the stage properties employed (*RHi*, IX (1902), 365-392, lines 93 SD, 127 SD, 160 SD; 225 SD, 269 SD; 881 SD, 908 SD).
[102] By A. Restori, in *RHi*, IX (1902), 357.

of the back-stage. This would indicate that the device, while already employed occasionally in staging practice, had not yet come into very general use.[103] In the *Farsa de Santa Bárbara* of Diego Sánchez de Badajoz[104] a shepherd is startled by the sudden *descubrimiento* of Christ, seated on a chair like a judge "con una cruz en la mano sobre un mundo" and "Santa Bárbara delante de él, bien ataviada" and "un Angel de la Guarda, que la lleva por la mano a juzgar" (p. 205). For the first part of the play this group remained in a kind of back-stage that was concealed from the spectators and from the rest of the stage by a curtain. Only when it was time for them to take part in the action were they disclosed to the shepherd and to the audience. The stage direction thus bringing the back-stage into use reads, "Aqui se descubre el Cristo y Santa Bárbara y el Angel, que están cubiertos con el pabellon" (p. 209).[105]

Other illustrations of a kind of back-stage are not utterly lacking. During the first part of the *Auto de la Resurrecion de Christo,* a curtain may have concealed an effigy of the Virgin.[106] In like manner, in the *Auto de la Asumption,*[107] the Virgin's house could be concealed from view. And the same method was used to reveal an *Ecce homo* in Lucas Fernández's *Auto de la Pasión* and probably also in the *Tres pasos de la Pasión.*[108] The back-stage in minia-

---

[103] Evidence of the appearance of a back-stage in the fifteenth century is limited to the use of a curtain to conceal the bed of the Virgin in the Catalonian Assumption play (see above, p. 21). When the curtain was closed, however, the setting for the Virgin did not entirely disappear, and it is doubtful whether this device was more than an approximation to a true back-stage. The *telones* employed in the Christmas play at Zaragoza in 1487 may possibly have been put to a similar use (Cañete, *Teatro español,* 94 n.).

[104] *Recopilación,* I, 205 ff.

[105] One would like to think that the chapel in the Cathedral of Badajoz which contains an altar dedicated to Santa Bárbara (López Prudencio, *Diego Sánchez de Badajoz,* 77-78) may have once served as the back-stage for Diego Sánchez's little play. We are told that Vicens García's Catalan play in the next century on the same subject "fou representada en la benediccó de la capella de la Santa" (García Silvestre, 315-316).

[106] Rouanet, *Colección,* IV, 295. The text is printed in Vol. II, Num. LX, 514-542. Performance undoubtedly took place at Easter, 1578 (cf. the *licencia,* pp. 541-542).

[107] See above, p. 83.

[108] See above, p. 76. Although there is no sign of a curtain in the *Ecce homo* printed by Paul Lefort and entitled École espagnole du XVᵉ siècle," the half-naked Christ does appear in a recess in the rear wall, which suggests a theatrical back-stage (*La peinture espagnole,* 43, Fig. 11).

ture may also have been quite frequent in the sacramental plays where the bread was hidden from the gaze of the audience by a small curtain.[109] And toward the end of the dramatic period before Lope de Vega, Cristóbal de Virués used what appears to be a full-fledged back-stage in three of his five plays. In the *Tragedia de la cruel Casandra,* a double door is opened and the dead bodies of Fabio, Principe and Fulgencia are revealed.[110] The *Elisa Dido* makes identical use of the back-stage, the dead body of Dido appearing when Iarbas opens the door.[111] And in the *Tragedia de la gran Semiramis,* although the body of the dead queen could have been off stage, it would seen that Virués was again employing his customary back-stage technique.[112]

In the texts of the *Pecador* and the other Nativity plays of the sixteenth century mentioned above, there is little specific authority for suggesting a back-stage. The stage direction in Timoneda's play, however, showing the sudden disclosure of the *Nacimiento,* is evidence that the device was surely used in this one play at least. To this may be added Alenda's account of an anonymous sixteenth century manuscript text, doubtfully attributed to Pedro Ramos. Alenda states that "al final 'se descubre el Santísimo nascimiento en la vara de Jesé, llena de Reyes, Patriarcas y Profetas, y en lo alto la Virgen Santísima María, con el niño Jesus, Salvador Nuestro, en los brazos: *todos vivos.* Y entretanto que está descubierto. . . .'"[113] Gil Vicente employed a back-stage at least as early as 1509 in his Castilian piece called *Auto de la Sibila Casandra.*[114] Part of the stage was entirely concealed until "Abrem se as cortinas onde estaa todo o aparato do nascimento . . ." (p. 37). From the accompanying dialogue the *aparato* must have included at least figures of the Mother and Child and possibly Joseph and

[109] Cf., e.g., the early *Farsa sacramental,* pub. by Serrano y Sanz, in *RABM,* X (1904), 450, and Diego Sánchez de Badajoz's *Farsa del Santísimo sacramento,* in *Recopilación,* II, pp. 36, 40.
[110] Pub. by Juliá Martínez, in *Poetas dramáticos valencianos,* I; see p. 90.
[111] *Ibid.,* pp. 174-175.
[112] *Ibid.,* p. 57b.
[113] "Catálogo," in *BRAE,* VI (1919), 758-759.
[114] Ed. Alvaro Giráldez, Madrid, 1931. Ticknor long ago noted the use of a back-stage in this play (*History of Spanish Literature,* I, 259).

the cradle. And finally additional evidence that the device of the back-stage was well known in the peninsula in the sixteenth century, if not yet in general use, may be found in two Portuguese plays. In Baltasar Diaz's *Auto do Nascimento,* the figures at the manger were placed in a similar back-stage, for at one point a stage direction reads, "Cerrarsehão as cortinas donde esta nossa Senhora."[115] And in another Portuguese Christmas play, the anonymous *Auto de deos padre & justiça & mia*[116] the back-stage is called a *portal* (iiija, verso) or *portalejo* ([Biiij], recto). It opens twice, as the stage directions indicate : 1) "descobrese o nacimento : & aparece Christo nascido : & adora ho nossa senhora dizendo . . ." ([Bj], recto) ; 2) "Abrirã o nacimēto . . ." ([Bj], verso).

Although the back-stage was often used independently, in some instances it formed part of a multiple stage. In the *Auto de la Asumption,* the Virgin's house was one of two or three simultaneous settings.[117] The *Ecce homo* in the *Tres pasos* was also used on a multiple stage. And in the Vicente Sibyl play the shepherds "vam cantando em chacota & chegando ao presepio, . . ." (p. 39). They are thus directed specifically to move from their original location to the manger setting, and this direction occurs in the text two pages later than the direction for opening the back-stage. A similar movement is required in the *Auto de deos padre* ([Avij], verso SD). In this play, however, there is additional evidence of the multiple stage in the fact that for a time two locations are in constant and simultaneous use. Isaiah and Zachariah converse on one part of the stage, while Mary and Joseph talk together at the *portal* (iiija, recto ff.). In the Baltasar Diaz play the connection of the back-stage with the multiple system is even more precise. For, in addition to the manger setting, the stage was decorated with a mansion for Jerusalem ([Axij], recto, SD), containing a chair for Herod (Aiiij, recto, SD; [Axij], verso, SD). There was also a special location for the shepherds (Aij,

---

[115] C. Michaëlis, *Autos portugueses,* fol. [Axiij], verso.
[116] Professor Gillet very kindly lent me his photostatic copy of the text, which is in the Biblioteca Nacional at Lisbon.
[117] Cf. above, p. 83.

verso, SD (sleep); [Ajx], recto, SD and Dialogue), where they made a fire to cook their meal and to warm themselves ([Aj], verso, SD; [Ajx], recto),[118] as well as one for the Emperor Augustus Caesar, who appeared in another place while the shepherds were asleep on the stage at their own location. Thus the stage was constantly multiple, and while the *portal* was on view there were simultaneous settings.[119]

Since Castilian performances in the sixteenth century occasionally used a back-stage, since the back-stage provided a regular method of performing Christmas plays in Portugal, and since the same device eventually came into general use in the seventeenth century, it is at least possible that the *portal* of the Castilian Nativity plays may have been represented by a back-stage. If so, it is difficult to determine whether they would have continued to use a multiple stage. If there was no setting at the shepherd's location, if the *portal* setting was not visible while the shepherd's location was in use, or if no shepherd remained there later while the *portal* was on view, in order to retain the identity of the loca-

---

[118] Although a stage fire may frequently have been imaginary, we find incontrovertible evidence that it was represented by some stage property in Diego Sánchez de Badajoz's *Farsa Racional del Libre Albedrío* (*Recopilación*, I, pp. 415 SD's, 418), Maestro Ferruz's *Auto de Cain y Abel* (Rouanet, *Colección*, II, Num. XLI (pp. 150-166), 95 SD, 106-108, 111-112), the anonymous *Entremés sin título* (Cotarelo, *Colección*, I, p. 59 SD's), and Juan de la Cueva's *Comedia de la Libertad de Roma por Mucio Cevola* (*Comedias y Tragedias*, II, Jornada III, pp. 395-397; Jornada IV, p. 357 (*Argumento*), 405 (*Argumento*), 414, and possibly 412-413). Fires are at least imagined in Juan del Encina, *Egloga de las grandes lluvias*, in *Teatro completo de Juan del Encina*, ed. Cañete, p. 140; Lucas Fernández, *Auto o Farsa del Nascimiento*, in *Farsas y Eglogas*, p. 179; Gil Vicente, *Farça chamada "Auto da India,"* in *Obras*, II, p. 266; Esteban Martín, *Auto, como San Juan fue concebido*, in *RR*, XVII (1926), 41-64, lines 334, 386 ff.; Bartolomé Aparicio, *Obra del Pecador*, in Gallardo, *Ensayo*, I, 233; anon., *Aucto del Martyrio de Sancta Eulalia*, in Rouanet, *Colección*, II, Num. XXXVIII (pp. 90-109), 565 SD: this and the other atrocities may have been performed off-stage (361, 396, 398, 541, 581); anon., *Entremés sin título*, in Cotarelo, *Colección*, I, p. 75 SD's).

[119] Baltasar Díaz wrote another play, the *Auto de Santa Caterina* (C. Michaëlis, *Autos portugueses*) in which three simultaneous settings definitely appear: (*a*) a mansion for St. Catherine, called an *estancia* (Aiiij, verso, SD; Avj, recto, SD; [Axiij], verso, SD). (*b*) A mansion for the prison [Ajx], recto, SD; [Axiij], verso, SD). (*c*) a mansion for the empress ([Axjv], recto, SD). If the place where the tortures were administered was different from the prison, the stage contained a fourth setting ([Axij], recto, SD; [Axvj], recto, SD). In addition, the emperor had a particular location ([Ajx], verso, SD; [Ax], recto, SD; [Axiij], verso, SD), which may perhaps have been decorated (Av, verso, SD; Avij, verso, SD); and another location was required for the hermitage (Aij verso; Aiij, recto, SD; Av, recto and verso, Dialogue, and verso, SD).

tion, then a multiple stage was probably not used. The violation of any one of these conditions, however, would assure the use of a multiple stage. Furthermore, if the actors definitely moved from one spot on the stage to another and if this movement involved a foreshortening of space as would be implied by the passage from the country to the city of Bethlehem, the stage must have been multiple. This, at least, is what seems to have happened in the *Obra del Pecador* and the other Nativity plays. They therefore used a multiple stage even when the *portal* was disclosed in a back-stage. The introduction of the back-stage into these multiple stages, as a substitute for a mansion that was on view throughout the performance, was doubtless of great influence in the simplification of the multiple system.[120]

C.

Another small group of four plays resembles the *Égloga de la Resurrección* in a modified fashion. Like the *Égloga* these plays require 1) simultaneous locations and 2) stage decoration at one of the locations. The stage decoration consists, however, of an entrance to a subterranean well, pit or grave. This was represented by a hole in the stage floor and thus involved the use of a lower level, presumably invisible and therefore not really part of a vertical multiple stage.[120a] But since another location, apparently undecorated, was employed on the earth level in addition to the opening in the floor, these plays did utilize a horizontal multiple stage.

This group of plays includes the following:

18. *Aucto de quando Jacob fue huyendo a las tierras de Aran*[121]

Two locations: *a*) just outside Laban's dwelling (72 ff., 170, 180, 381 ff.), and *b*) a section of the country (183 ff.) containing a

---

[120] Cf. Fischel's description of the Amsterdam "Schonburgh" ("Art and the Theatre," 60).
[120a] See above, pp. 55-56.
[121] Rouanet, *Colección*, I, Num. IV, 51-66.

well (289, 291 SD-294, 299, 304-308). Rachel's return to her father and Jacob's subsequent arrival involve the simultaneous presence of both locations (363, 370, 370 SD, 381-384). The pine tree imagined as decoration for the road between them (381-384) may be merely spoken scenery, since the action makes no use of it.

19. Aucto de quando Sancta Elena hallo la cruz de Nuestro Señor[122]

Two locations. a) Queen Helen's stopping place a day's journey from Jerusalem (77-79), and b) Jerusalem. Action passing back and forth bewteen them and requiring their simultaneous presence is frequent (86 ff., 104-106, 145-146, 300 SD). The stopping place contained a well (pozo) as setting (411-414, 436-438, 441-455 SD), which may have served later as the hiding place for the three crosses (513, 531, 536-537, 544-547, 555, 562, 595 SD, 599-600 SD, 605 and SD). A special location for the emperor (1-75 SD) is uncertain, although there is some suggestion of the use of mansions (165 SD).[123]

20. Auto de los desposorios de Ysac[124]

Two locations: a) Batuel's home, and b) the place in the country where Eliazer met Rebecca, which is at least imagined to contain a fuente (200 SD, 204-210, 231-232, 249, 328, 369, 618, 644-645). The coexistence of the two and travel between them on the stage is obligatory (338-342, 346-348, 351-353).

21. Aucto de la Visitaçion de Sant Antonio a Sant Pablo[125]

Probably two locations: a) St. Paul's dwelling, called a cueva (138), with an entrance puerta (148), and b) St. Anthony's hermitage (hermita: 249, 277 SD, 393 SD). Shifts of action occur

[122] Ibid., II, Num. XXXIII, 21-42.
[123] Cf. above, p. 92 and n. 78.
[124] Rouanet, Colección, I, Num. V, 67-90.
[125] Ibid., III, Num. LXXVI, 261-275. This auto may have been performed at Seville in 1570 (ibid., IV, 329; Sánchez-Arjona, Anales, 43).

frequently between the two (249-250, 277 SD, 393 SD). The grave in which St. Paul is buried is doubtless a part of his location (368 SD, 373 SD, 374-379).

D.

Five other plays illustrate the staging method of the *Égloga de la Resurrección* with other slight differences in the setting. Conforming to type, these plays again used simultaneous locations with stage decoration at one of them. A wide variety of settings seems to have been available, however, and different stage decoration was required for the performance of each of the following texts:

22. *Tragedia de los amores de Eneas y de la Reyna Dido*[126]

Two locations: *a*) Jupiter's position and *b*) Carthage—in Jornada III (1066-1111). Carthage was decorated in Jornada V with a tower (2450-2460, 2485-2488, 2500-2501). The action of Jornada II may occur at a single place (the garden), as may also that of Jornada V, where the scene is outside Dido's castle. Several different places of action appear in both Jornada I and Jornada IV, but they may appear consecutively and not necessarily at the same time, since every change is accompanied by a momentarily empty stage or by a complete turnover in the personnel of the actors on stage (J. I, 354-355, 450-451; J. IV, 1889 SD, 1997-1998. In Jornada III, however, the multiple stage is essential.

23. Juan de Pedraza, An Easter-Play[127]

In addition to an off-stage Limbo, probably at the entrance to the choir for the *Parte primera* (see above, n. 67), two locations in

---

[126] Ed. Gillet and Williams, in *PMLA*, XLVI (1931), 353-431. The editors date the work between 1536 and 1546.
[127] Ed. Gillet, in *RHi*, LXXXI¹ (1933), 550-607. The play was probably performed on Easter morning and in church (*ibid.*, pp. 551-552), possibly about the middle of the century, since the title page bears the date 1549 and editions of Pedraza's other two known works, *Comedia de Sancta Susaña* and *Farsa llamada Dança de la muerte* appeared in 1551 (Moratín, *Orígenes*, I, 179; González Pedroso, *BAE*, LVIII. 41 n. 1).

the remainder of the play: *a*) one for the Virgin Mary (322 SD, 1021 SD), and *b*) the other decorated with a tomb (*monumento:* 645 SD, 686-700, 738-741, 755-756, 772-773, 917 SD, 1005 SD, 1061 SD), apparently large enough for a man to walk into (934-936). This spacious structure may have been elaborately wrought, possibly even just such an attempted imitation of the Original Holy Sepulchre at Jerusalem as was frequently found elsewhere in Europe.[128] Characters frequently move between Mary's location and the tomb (441 SD, 501 SD, 1022-1037, 1061 SD), doubtless along the intervening roadway where the other two Marys awaited the Magdalene (917 SD, 1102-1103, 1117 SD). The Virgin's location may have been a mansion in which personages could be concealed from the audience (645 SD), just as in the tomb (441 SD).

24. *Auto del sacreficio de Abraham*[129]

Two locations: *a*) the place where Abraham and Isaac leave the Bobo Rrecuenco (453-459) and to which they subsequently return (598-599, 602-604, 607); and *b*) outside Abraham's home (120, 408 ff.), which is temporarily furnished with table and chairs (191 SD-193, 295 SD-297, 301 ff., 373-377) and which may later be used as the place for the sacrifice (478-479), equipped with an altar, perhaps constructed on the stage and especially for the occasion by Abraham and his son (466-470, 480-481, 526 SD, 567 SD). If the sacrifice scene[130] took place at a different location from that which represented Abraham's home, a three-location technique was employed. Since Rrecuenco was left along the road, the stage might have consisted of two settings with an intervening

---

[128] See Young, *The Drama of the Medieval Church*, II, 400, 507-513; also the studies of Brooks and Bonnell (cf. Bibliography).

[129] Rouanet, *Colección*, I, Num. I, 1-21. Corpus Christi plays on Abraham were performed at Seville in 1560 and 1571 (*ibid.*, IV, 136), and one on the sacrifice was presented in a Majorcan church some time during the century (Llabrés, "Repertorio," in *RABM*, V (1901), 920 ff., Num. 26).

[130] In *Juanita la Larga* (Chapter XXXVI) Juan Valera describes a modern Andalusian *auto* on Abraham and Isaac given in Holy Week. The setting includes a *monte* which "está representado en medio de la plaza por un tablado cubierto de verdura."

roadway such as was supplied later by the two *carros* and connecting trestles.

25. *Auto de la destruicion de Jerusalen*[131]

Three locations for *a*) the emperor, *b*) Jerusalem and *c*) Pilate. The seneschal moves from *a*) to *b*) (101-102, 111-115 SD, 127), and from *b*) to *c*) (229-231 SD), after which personages are present simultaneously at all three. The seneschal returns from *c*) to *b*) (281-284), and thence to *a*) (291 ff., 300 SD-306). Other shifts from *c*) to *b*) are effected by Archelao (505 SD, 535-536, 565 SD) and Pilate himself (606-611), and from *a*) to *b*) by the emperor, and his retinue (395). Jerusalem contains a stage setting for a wall (395 SD-405, 420, 426-430, 435 SD),[132] which may have had near it or under it a passageway for an exit (436, 455 SD, 465 SD, 505 SD, 654 SD), once called *puerta* (420). It is not unlikely that the emperor's location was furnished with a chair or throne and that Pilate was seated on his judiciary bench.[133]

26. *Auto de la entrada de Xpo en Jerusalen*[134]

Three locations for: *a*) the original position of Christ and his disciples, *b*) the place called a *castillo* (33) where the animals (*asna* and *pollino*) were stationed, and *c*) the temple, in addition to a roadway (165 SD-211). So closely and intricately interwoven are the parts of the action at the different locations that a few textual citations for each are inadequate. For example, one bit of evidence for the separateness of *b*) and *c*), as well as for some structural setting for *c*), lies in the fact that the first temple scene follows the *asna* scene and proceeds for eighteen verses before the place of action—*tenplo*—is mentioned (135). The spectator does not see or hear the stage direction that aids the reader and which places the action "en el tenplo" (117), and unless it took place on

---

[131] Rouanet, *Colección*, I, Num. XXX, 502-524.
[132] For other plays utilizing a wall as part of their stage setting, see Shoemaker, 306-308, 311-313, 318.
[133] Pharaoh was accorded a chair in the *Tragedia Josephina* (see above, p. 78), as also was Herod in the *Aucto de la prisión de San Pedro* (see above, p. 93).
[134] Rouanet, *Colección*, II, Num. XLVI, 264-278.

a separate location, the spectator will still be thinking of the place as that belonging to the two animals. The following passages are suggested, however, as among the most significant: 31-38, 47 ff., 79-81, 91 ff., 117 SD, 137 SD-141. The setting for the temple consisted of various kinds of portable materials put up as shops by the traders (117 SD-124, 128-129) and probably some structure simulating a building (240-241, 243 SD, 259 SD, 278, 299). Decoration for the animals' location is possible, for they are said to be tied (55, 78) and fed (77, 86).[135]

E.

Several other plays employed a multiple stage, for which stage decoration is not clearly indicated in the texts. In this respect the locations are similar to those indicated for Mary and Jesus respectively in the *Égloga de la Resurrección*. For although the locations for Christ and His mother may not have been decorated at all, they were necessarily separate and distinct and were in simultaneous use. In the following plays a like situation exists. Settings and decoration may sometimes be suggested; but even if they were certain, it would not be clear what relation they had with the multiple stage technique.

27. Comedia a lo Pastoril para la noche de Navidad[136]

Two locations in the third *Nocturno* for: *a*) Verbo Eterno and *b*) Amor. Hombre and Deseo leave Verbo, seek and find Amor, and send him to where they had left Verbo. Amor follows their directions and is greeted by Verbo on his arrival (911-912, 944-955, 978, 982, 988-990, 1169-1170, 1174-1175). There is also some suggestion of other locations. The first scene of the play ends as Hombre falls asleep on the stage (138-139). In Estancias I and II, which follow, he takes no part in the action.

---

[135] The term for this location, *castillo*, may mean simply village (cf. Timoneda's *Aucto del castillo de Emaus*, ed. Johnson, pp. 15 ff. and 15 n. 1).

[136] Pub. by Crawford, in *RHi*, XXIV (1911), 497-541. The *Comedia* was probably performed in church, or just outside, early Christmas morning either before or after the matins service, between the years 1550 and 1575 (Crawford, *ibid.*, 497-498).

The four Virtues wake him at the opening of Estancia III. Presumably Hombre remained asleep on the stage while Estancias I and II were presented. The action of these two was imagined to occur in places quite other than Hombre's resting spot. Some of these places may have been a location for the three sisters Truth, Pity and Peace (378 ff.) and one for Diuinidad that was equipped with a chair (348). In the fourth *Nocturno* of this play stage setting may have decorated a special location for a *nacimiento* with its *portal* and cradle (1346-1350, 1372-1373, 1391-1393, 1436-1441, 1453, 1456-1459).

28. *Aucto de la Ungion de David*[137]

Two locations: a) the original position of Samuel and his servant, and b) Bethlehem (96-97, 104-105 SD, 115-121, 130 SD, 131-132, 156-161, 271, 294 SD, 355, 375 SD, 376-378). The first place at which the *viejos* appeared may very likely have been a third location (130 SD). An altar was built at Bethlehem (151-155 SD, 184) for the sacrifice of the *bezerro* (105 SD, 155 SD), but there is no certainty that it remained longer than the particular scene in which it was built.[138]

29. *Sebastián de Horozco, Representación de la famosa historia de Ruth*[139]

Two locations: a) an indefinite place just outside the city of Bethlehem, and b) a field (p. 202, col. 2 Dialogue and SD). Other possible but uncertain settings and locations are suggested (pp.

[137] Rouanet, *Colección*, I, Num. XIX, 315-330. The play contains a prose *argumento* in which an appeal for "El acostunbrada atençion" is made to the "Illustre *auditorio*" (p. 315).
[138] Cf. also above, p. 92 and n. 78.
[139] The fragmentary text appears in the *Cancionero de Sebastian de Horozco*, pub. by Soc. de bib. and., Sevilla, 1874, pp. 195-207. It is known that two of Horozco's four extant plays were performed in Toledo, one of them in 1548 (pp. 148, 167). His expressed concern for the performance of the Ruth play is noticeable in two items which appear in an explanation of the piece which the author himself has inserted between title and text: ". . . y por dar gusto á los oyentes," and "y para la representacion, y porque se diferenciasen en lo que cada una de ellas dize, les pusimos nombres Lia y Cetura, aunque la historia no las nombre sino diziendo *mulieres*" (p. 195).

200-1 SD's; 204-1 SD). The consecutive stage technique could have sufficed for the first half of the play (pp. 195-200, col. 1).

In the two secular plays that follow it is not entirely clear whether or not the distance separating the places of action was great enough to necessitate imaginative foreshortening.[140] These two plays are therefore included only provisionally.

30. Diego de Ávila, *Egloga interlocutoria*[141]

Possibly two locations for: *a*) the luncheon in the *encinar*, and *b*) Tenorio's nap (122, 207-208 SD, 376 SD).

31. Juan de París, *Egloga*[142]

Possibly two locations for: *a*) the position of Cremon Repicado, Estacio and *doncella* at the start of their journey, and *b*) the hermitage at the end of it (7, 58, 271, 475-480, 495-506).

III

Dramatic texts of the sixteenth century yield evidence of their staging which, even at best, is incomplete. In spite of the lack of completeness in this kind of evidence many plays have revealed the need of a multiple stage technique for their performance. It is reasonable to suppose therefore that many other plays whose texts are still less clear in staging requirements may have been performed on a multiple stage. A few such texts will now be discussed very briefly, in so far as their possible relations with such a stage are concerned.

The texts which follow are of two different kinds. The first

---

[140] Such a situation also obtains in the anonymous Portuguese *Farsa Penada* (1542 or earlier) where three positions for a dead *dōzela*, a sleeping *paruo*, and a newly arrived *moço* were used simultaneously (C. Michaëlis, *Autos portugueses*, Aiiij, recto, col. 1 SD-verso, col. 2 SD).

[141] Kohler, *Sieben spanische dramatische Eklogen*, 236-266. The first edition was prior to 1512 (Kohler, 168).

[142] [Urban Cronan], *Teatro español del siglo XVI*, Madrid, 1913, I, 391 ff.

three plays could be admirably performed according to the multiple stage method, and although the texts do not absolutely require it there is some reason to suppose that this method may have been used. The texts of the last three plays however contain no adequate reason to warrant a multiple stage although certain superficial features in each one might appear to suggest it. Many more problematical plays of both types doubtless exist.[143] These six may be considered illustrative of border-line cases in general, plays which, with our present incomplete evidence, hover between a multiple and a single stage.

1. *Aucto de Sant Christobal.*[144]

The action of this play took place first in the presence of the King (1 SD-110), then in the open, rocky country (111-305, especially 179-182 ff.), and finally at the edge of a river (306-490). These three places could have been imagined successively on one location. But there are two suggestive features in the text, each of which, if accepted, would necessitate a multiple stage. These features are *a*) a possible special location or setting for the King and *b*) a body of water to represent the river.

The opening stage direction of the play, "Entra San Xpoval dond' esta el Rrey," may mean that the King was seated on a throne. After St. Christopher takes leave of him, the King delivers a short monologue, during which the saint moves to the open, rocky country. There is no indication of exit and reëntrance by St. Christopher, and none indeed for the King, who may then have remained at his location during the entire play.

In the third scene the giant saint ferried a Portuguese, an old woman and her two sons (*bobos*), and finally Our Savior across the river in three different trips. He seems to have carried them on

---

[143] E.g., Palau's *Farsa Salamantina* (*BHi*, II (1900), 242 ff.), where two different locations could have been used for Salamantina's and Mencía's houses; and Encina's *Egloga de Cristino y Febea* (*Teatro completo*, 379-409), where a single location probably represented Amor's location and Cristino's hermitage in succession (p. 394).

[144] Rouanet, *Colección*, I, Num. XXVII. The considerable popularity of the theme increases the likelihood that our present text was performed (*ibid.*, IV, 203-205; Mérimée, *L'art dramatique*, 25; Llabrés, "Repertorio," in *RABM*, V (1901), 920 ff., Num. 32, 33). Cf. above also, p. 16.

112 THE MULTIPLE STAGE IN SPAIN

his shoulders as he is customarily pictured in the fine arts.[145] But on the second trip, when he took the two boys along with their mother, farcical elements were introduced. He carried one boy under each arm, and occasionally dangled them into the water (401-403). The dialogue frequently suggests that a real body of water was present, through which St. Christopher was wading back and forth with his passengers. The Portuguese had been splashed with water (358-363) but now the old lady has lost her shoes and she and the boys are drenched (411-425). All this may have been mere pantomine and imagination, and the water merely "spoken scenery." But it is difficult to see in such a performance the farcical effect of boisterous laughter which the author obviously sought in this scene. The apparatus was so much simpler than that used in other known dramatic and non-dramatic uses of a body of water[146] that we cannot admit insuperable material difficulties as an objection to its adoption into the staging of this play.

If decoration appeared on the stage for the river, the first two parts of the play must have been enacted on a different location. And if the King and his throne were also present throughout the play, a third location may even have been necessary for the scene in the open country. This place may indeed have been represented by the neutral space between and in front of the two settings. It is evident that the use of a multiple stage for this *Auto* rests upon

[145] Calvert, *Escorial*, plate 207.

[146] In 1570 a huge pool was built in Madrid and used as the scene for spectacular naval battles in the festivities held at the entrance of Philip II's second wife, Dª Ana de Austria, into the city (Alenda, *Relaciones de solemnidades,* I, 79, Num. 258). A similar device seems to have been employed at Denia-Valencia in 1599 for the entertainment offered to Philip III and Dª Isabel Clara (*ibid.,* 120, Num. 411). More details are available concerning the *mar* employed at Plasencia in 1578 for the Corpus Christi *Auto* on Jonas: ". . . se hizo en medio de la plaza un gran tablado, que parecia hecho para muchos días, y en lo alto un mar de sesenta pies de longitud y veinte de latitud, con abundancia de agua que con mucho artificio habían hecho subir allí" (Sánchez-Arjona, *Anales,* 97 n. 1). Five of Gil Vicente's plays and one imitation employ boats, but we cannot be sure that they were floated in or surrounded by water, although the practice had a precedent in Italy, since a performance of the *Menaechmi* at Ferrara in 1486 included a practicable boat which moved with "dieci persone dentro con remi et vela" (d'Ancona, II, 128). Less literal elaborateness of settings was employed in the next century, when perspective in painting was brought from Italy to the aid of the Spanish stage. Cosme Lotti's decoration for Lope de Vega's *La selva sin amor* included "un mar en perspectiva" (*BAE,* XXXVIII, 300).

the admission of either of two hypothetical elements in the staging. The use of these elements in other sixteenth century performances shows, however, that this *Auto* is not a unique, isolated instance of such settings. A multiple stage, therefore, while by no means obligatory, would have provided a possible and a most appropriate *mise en scène* for the *Aucto de Sant Christobal*.

2. Bartolomé Palau, *Victoria Christi*[147]

The greater part of this play could have been performed on a single location before the entrance to Limbo. Auto 3° of Parte I is somewhat more complicated and, like the *Aucto de Sant Christobal*, makes use of three or four different places of action—the place where Abel persuaded Cain to offer some sacrifice to God, the place of sacrifice to which they went, the position of Lucifer and Culpa, and the entrance to Limbo. These places were used consecutively in the above order, and no two of them were used simultaneously. Since it is not certain that settings appeared on the stage, a single location would have sufficed to represent all these places in succession. If Lucifer were seated as he sometimes was,[148] the chair or throne may have been placed before the entrance to Limbo, and thus formed a part of the location. If Lucifer were on the stage, however, either seated or standing at his location, during the persuasion and the sacrifice scenes, then the stage was multiple. Also if a permanent or fixed altar appeared

[147] Victoria Christi nvevamente compvesta por el Bachiller Bartolome Palau, natural de Burbaguena, . . . En Barcelona, en casa de Antonio La cavalleria en la calle de los libreros, Año 1670. A collation of this edition with the Autos 1°, 3°, and 5° of Parte I which Rouanet published from the 1570 edition (*Colección*, IV, 374-394) reveals important variants, but none which in any way affects the technique or the decoration in the presentation of the play. This amorphous play, with no evident breaks or pauses in the action between *Autos* or *Partes,* displays considerable similarity in structure to the *Danza de la Muerte.* Abel, Noe, Abrahan, Joseph, Moysen, Auaricio, Sanson and Bobo, David, Solomon, and Judith are all in turn received by Lucifer, Satanás, and Culpa and sent into Limbo. The only appreciable variations from the procession type of construction are in the first part on original sin and the last on the redemption. For performances of this play and its influence in Catalonian territory in the seventeenth century, see Pons, 270-274, 320-321. The first part is similar to the older Valencian Adam and Eve play (*ibid.,* 239; cf. also above, pp. 16-18).
[148] Cf. above, p. 88.

on the stage for the sacrifices, the stage must have been multiple, for the altar and the entrance to Limbo necessarily represented widely separated places. The boys' remarks concerning God's acceptance of Abel's sacrifice (p. 9, verso, col. 1) and the manner of his acceptance "con fuego" (9, v., 2) follow some time after the implied action. They may refer, however, to the descent of an *araceli* to an altar upon which the sacrifices had been placed. This is what happened in Maestro Ferruz's *Auto de Cain y Abel*,[149] which deals with this very part of the *Victoria Christi* theme.

3. *Aucto del hijo pródigo*[150]

The places of action are: a) home, b)-d) various spots where Pródigo's successive experiences with the Portuguese and his dogs, the *Muger enamorada,* and the Porquero occurred and e) home again. These places may have been represented in succession on a single location without settings. If a multiple stage had been available however, one location would have represented "home," and at least one other besides the neutral space would have been used for the various episodes in Pródigo's wayward life.

In the following plays the multiple stage is rejected, because the indications of such a method of performance are more apparent than real:

4. Juan de Pedraza, *Farsa llamada Danza de la Muerte*[151]

A multiple stage is suggested by stage directions which speci-

---

[149] Rouanet, *Colección*, II, Num. XLI (pp. 150-166), 95 SD, 105-112. Whether or not the *mise en scène* suggested by Mérimée (*L'art dramatique*, 228-230) was really employed for a performance of this play, it is extremely doubtful whether the necessary staging constituted a multiple stage.

[150] Rouanet, *Colección*, II, Num. XLVIII. Mariscal de Gante says that this theme was "uno de los asuntos más tratados en el drama sacramental" (*Los autos sacramentales*, 124). Cf. also Rouanet, *Colección,* IV, 261. Two Prodigal Son plays were performed in Majorca, inside the church in the sixteenth century or earlier, according to Llabrés ("Repertorio," in *RABM*, V (1901), 921, Num. 13 and 14).

[151] *BAE*, LVIII, 41-46. It was written for a Corpus Christi celebration (p. 46), is entirely capable of being performed, and in the Introito Pastor constantly refers to "auditor," "noble auditorio" (pp. 41b, 42b, 46b).

fically designate four different places of action—for the first two *escenas* a "camara en un palacio del Papa" (p. 42, col. 1), for the third and fourth an "aposento régio" (42-2), for the next two "un camarin" (43-1), and for the remainder of the play a "monte" (43-2). But there is no other indication of stage decoration and no hint that setting or properties of any kind were used in the action of the play. Furthermore, the places indicated by the four stage directions appeared in succession and never simultaneously. Since the stage was completely cleared of players at every change in the place of action,[152] there was no need for one place to remain visible while action was in progress at another, and no need for movements on the stage from one location to another. It seems likely therefore that the four stage directions merely intend to designate what place the stage is imagined to represent at the time.[153] The changes in the place of action were therefore entirely imaginary and never involved more than one location.

5. *Aucto de la Paciencia de Job*[154]

Satan and Job's wife Arabisa are on a different part of the stage from that occupied by Job himself, and Arabisa moves from one spot to the other (447, 455-457). There is no suggestion, however, that the distance between them was any greater in the imagination than it was in reality. The stage contains one slightly extended but continuous location representing a street (429). There is no evidence that the stage space was imaginatively foreshortened. From this text no artificial divisions of the stage could be created, either by scenery or by the imagination.

---

[152] "Vase" (42-1), "Entranse" (42-2), "Vanse" (43-1), "Vanse" (43-2).

[153] For other examples of stage directions which cannot be admitted as proof of the existence of stage decoration because they are not confirmed by the action, cf. three plays of Timoneda: *Aucto de la oveja perdida* (ed. García Boiza, Salamanca, 1921, especially 125 SD); *Aucto de la Fee* (ed. González Pedroso, *BAE*, LVIII, especially p. 89b, first part); *Obra llamada los desposorios de Cristo*, *ibid.*, especially p. 104b ("Campo"), and p. 105b (Estancia régia").

[154] Rouanet, *Colección*, IV, Num. XCVI, 105-127.

6. Francisco de las Cuebas, *Representación de
los mártires Justo y Pastor*[155]

For the first staging of this three-part performance at Alcalá de
Henares in 1568 an itinerant performance was planned.[156] The
funeral procession was to stop at three different stations, and one
act of the play was to be presented at each: Act I on an elaborate
carro (pp. 431-433), two hundred paces outside the Puerta de los
Mártires where a magnificent *túmulo*[157] had been erected; Act II
inside the city at San Juan de la Penitencia as soon thereafter as
possible; and Act III later "en al altar de la lonja.[158] This plan was
not carried out completely because, before the end of Act II was
reached, the hour grew too late to continue. Nevertheless this kind
of presentation had been planned and must therefore be included
as one of the methods of performance.

The three different stations resemble the multiple stage method.
But the similarity is remote and superficial for it is evident that at
no time did the audience behold simultaneous horizontal locations
or settings; at no time did it have a panoramic view of the three
settings. The spectators moved, when the settings moved, from
stage to stage, as they did in England for the procession plays[159]

---

[155] Pub. by Crawford, in *RHi*, XIX (1908), 431 ff. This text has sometimes been
considered one play and sometimes three (Cañete, *Teatro español*, 311; Alenda,
"Catálogo," 496). Suffice it to say that Ambrosio de Morales, chronicler of the festivities,
writes of the three *actos* as three different *representaciones* (*La vida, el martyrio,
la inuencion, las grandezas, y las translaciones de los gloriosos niños martyres san
Iusto y Pastor, y el solenne triumpho con que fueron recebidas sus santas Reliquias
en Alcalá de Henares en su postrera translacion*, fols. 134, recto ff. There is a copy
of this rare work in the library of the Hispanic Society of America.) Morales was
undoubtedly an eyewitness since his account appeared so soon after the event (cf.
García López, *Ensayo de una tipografía complutense*, Num. 426, p. 135a). Certainly
no organic unity exists between the three parts, each of which, like those of the
Tres pasos de la pasión, has its own *argumento*, and the second even its own special
plea for the spectator's attention (p. 441).
[156] García Icazbalceta records a similar technique in Mexico in the year 1538.
For the Corpus Christi festivities there seem to have been four stations "en cuatro
esquinas ó vueltas que se hacian en el camino, en cada una su montaña, y de cada
una salia un peñon bien alto" (*Coloquios espirituales y sacramentales de Fernán
González de Eslava*, xi), and on St. John the Baptist's day there were four different
tablados or *cadalsos* for as many *autos* in as many different parts of the city (*ibid.*,
xii ff.).
[157] Described by Morales, fol. 90r.
[158] Alenda, "Catálogo," 503.
[159] Chambers, *Mediaeval Stage*, II, 95 ff.

and in Germany for a Corpus Christi performance in Künselsau which was similarly divided between three different stations.[160] The magnificent *carro* traveled, for example, away from the *túmulo*, which marked the place for Act I but which performed no function whatever in the representation, passed "algo adelante de la procision" and "benia á ponerse debaxo del susodicho cielo ... " (p. 441), and the stage was now set for Act II. A similar shift of audience and stage settings was intended for the relatively simple Act III.

The second presentation of the *Justo y Pastor* play took place on March 15, a week later than the itinerant performance, and this time the work was performed in its entirety inside the church of San Justo. The stage used for Act II must have more than satisfied all the requirements of all three acts, and this stage never represented more than one horizontal location at a time. Every effort was made to present on this one location an exact reproduction of the previous week's performance, which had been spread out over three stations. It does not seem to have been especially difficult because the earth setting had been a single *carro* moving from stage to stage. On the fifteenth the functionless *túmulo* was duplicated by another tomb[161] in San Justo, the same movable *carro* was retained, and one act after another unfolded "debaxo la gran nuue que estaua puesta entre los dos coros, y el *castillo debaxo.*"[162]

In neither of these two different performances, then, was a multiple horizontal stage either planned or used. In both, the earth level was always a single location. Even during the second performance this location may possibly have moved between Act II and III to a position under "el arco triumphal que se hizo á la puerta de la iglesia" (*argumento*, p. 446), although there is no real need for this transfer in the action of Act III. But even if it did take place, the move is obviously just another manifestation of the original

[160] Creizenach, I, 233-234.
[161] Described by Morales, fols. 130v-131r.
[162] *Ibid.*, fol. 141v. The prose introduction to the play calls the *carro* also a "castillo mouedizo."

itinerant technique. For it must be very doubtful whether the spectators could view both the elaborate Heaven inside the church and the triumphal arch at the doorway at the same time and without changing their position.[163]

From the available evidence on methods of performance it is possible to conclude that the horizontal multiple stage definitely continued and persisted in the sixteenth century. With many Castilian texts now available, the quantitative evidence of this kind of staging is considerable. Statistical computations must be of very dubious worth on account of the scantiness of documentary evidence and the inherent incompleteness of textual evidence. Nevertheless, even without any comparative estimate, the mere number of plays which require the horizontal multiple stage is striking indeed. Besides the five performances suggested by the documents, the texts of forty-two plays show definitely that they needed such a stage for their presentation. Nine other texts, tentatively grouped as provisional or doubtful, may also have been performed by this method. And many more plays, of which texts are lost, incomplete, or lacking in staging information, were also probably mounted on a multiple stage.

Of the forty-two texts, seventeen definitely require simultaneous settings (I : 1-17). of these seventeen, five must have used decoration at three or more locations (1, 2, 6, 16, 17) ; and the needs of only two plays are definitely limited to two settings (7, 14). The twenty-five other pieces (II : 1-6, 11-29) definitely require simultaneous locations. For twenty-two of them (1-6, 11-26) stage decoration is precisely indicated for at least one of the locations. Only three texts (27-29) fail utterly to demand setting of some kind.

No less striking than the quantitative evidence is the variety of settings that appeared in different combinations and associations on the horizontal multiple stage in the sixteenth century. These settings include a cross (I : 1, 2, 3, 5) ; a tomb (I : 1, 2, 5 (?), 6, 9 (?),

---

[163] The vertical multiple stage for this play has been discussed above, pp. 45-47.

10, 11; II: 23) an altar (I: 4; II: 24, 28 possibly; III: 2 possibly);
a house represented by a *pavellón* (I:4) or a *palacio* (I:15) and
once apparently suspended in the air (I:16); the entrance hole to
a well, pit or grave (I:6; II:18-21); the elevated window of a
house as if it were on the second floor (I:7, 8, 14); the entrance to
a cave (I:13; II:20 possibly); a temple (I:13 and a possibly 4;
II:26); a thicket concealing a bath (I:15; II:3 possibly); a tower
('San Hermenegildo' tragedy; I:16; II:22); a doorway or gateway
(II:11-17; I:1, 3 probably, 5; II:25 possibly), which may also have
been the kind of setting for the various sacraments in the Mexican
coloquios (I:16, 17); a wall ('San Hermenegildo' tragedy; II:25);
and possibly a body of water (III:1).

In addition to these structural settings, a number of stage properties were often employed as decoration on a multiple stage.
Chief among these properties were some sort of seat, bench or
group of chairs (I:1, 2, 3, 6, 8; II:1-6, 24; and possibly II:25, 27
and III:1, 2), a table (I:14; II:4 probably) and a bed (I:9, 10, 11,
14).

Only in the few documentary notices and in the Catalan texts is
there indication that scaffolds or platforms were used to support
these settings and properties. Indeed, descriptive features of the
stage decoration are meagre and are usually confined to items that
may be deduced from the use for which the scenery was intended.
Thus, the cross was large enough to bear the figure or effigy of a
man and the tomb long, narrow and flat, but large enough to accommodate the body of a grown person. The bed and chairs were
similarly of a practicable size. And the altar was, at least on one
occasion (II:24), large and strong enough to support the boy
Isaac. The temple was once a mansion supported by two columns
which are torn down by the mighty Samson (I:13).

Gates or doors may sometimes have decorated a mere exit, as
in the representation of an off-stage Limbo (II:1; etc.) and the
entrance to the city of Seville in the 'San Hermenegildo' tragedy.
Perhaps other exits were also represented by similar setting. The
doorway in Nativity plays, however, was probably a back-stage cov-

ered by a curtain. When it was opened it contained the figures of the Holy Family and became a visible location or setting.

The tendency of the multiple stage in the sixteenth century toward a simpler form than that which usually appeared earlier is frequently manifest. Twenty-two of the forty-two definite examples of this method need only one setting. For some of these twenty-two there is a strong likelihood that other locations were also decorated. And for many more, uncertainties and incompleteness in the textual evidence may conceal other settings. Nevertheless, these twenty-two could have been performed on a stage where only one location was equipped with setting. And even if other settings did appear, these twenty-two texts give more attention and importance to this lone setting and the location which it decorates than they do to the locations which may have been undecorated. Even in the plays where two or more simultaneous settings were definitely employed, greater importance was often attached to one setting than to the others as was true, for example, of the cross in the *Quinta Angustia.*

But there are other indications of this tendency toward simplification, which had first made its appearance in the late fifteenth century examples of the multiple stage. In the Assumption *autos* the stations in Mary's pilgrimage were totally eliminated, and the horizontal stage consisted of only two or at most three settings. The Nativity plays usually required only one setting, the Bethlehem *portal*, with no suggestion of the tree of Paradise and the towers of the Holy City which had appeared in fifteenth century Valencian performances.

Furthermore, the principle of imaginative foreshortening, which is fundamental to the multiple stage, was often noticeably weakened. In some plays of two locations, the undecorated one did not represent a specific place (II:5, 11-16). In these plays and many others (II:26, for example), although foreshortening was still necessary, it is by no means clear to what degree the imagination had to extend the few feet of stage. Indeed in some plays (II, 7-10,

30, 31), the foreshortening is so vague or obscure that they may be only provisionally included as examples of multiple staging.

The back-stage was also a factor in the simplification of the multiple stage, since it did not remain on view throughout an entire performance as did the other settings, but only during the scenes where it was employed in the action. In fact, by this means a simple stage of one location may sometimes have been employed instead of a multiple stage (Diego Sánchez de Badajoz, *Farsa de Santa Bárbara*). Certainly in the seventeenth century this device often sufficed in a play which would otherwise have required a multiple stage.

Besides frequent and perhaps general simplification, three other phenomena have been observed in connection with the multiple stage of the sixteenth century which were not encountered earlier. One is the extension of this method of staging to such semi-religious or morality plays as the *Comedia Pródiga*[164] and to such completely secular works as the *Auto de Clarindo*. The 'Dido and Eneas' tragedy utilized the multiple stage in a part of its performance at least, as did also perhaps the *Églogas* of Diego de Ávila and Juan de París (II :30, 31). A second phenomenon is the mingling in a single play of the multiple stage method with the consecutive stage technique. This occurrence is exemplified by the religious play on 'Ruth' as well as by the secular 'Dido and Eneas' tragedy. The third noteworthy phenomenon is the spread of multiple staging to new theaters. This factor is usually entirely unknown or very obscure. But for six of the plays discussed the theater was either definitely (I :4, 6, 16; II :3) or very probably (I :2, 14), outdoors and for the *Tres pasos* (I :3) it was doubtless the hall of a private palace. For the *Desposorios de Joseph*, (I :14) two *carros* are strongly suggested. The church has definitely ceased to be the exclusive theater for multiple staging.

The multiple stage was still essentially a technique for the

---

[164] For the late appearance in Spain of the Morality play, see Pons, 237; Valbuena, 15-16; Parker, 179.

performance of religious plays, and appeared in a highly developed form in a few plays like the *Quinta Angustia,* Carvajal's *Josephina,* the Mexican sacramental plays, and perhaps several others. But extension to secular plays, contamination with other techniques and the introduction of devices like the curtained back-stage combined to weaken the principles underlying the method. Consequently, while still manifest in a large number of plays and in considerable variety of detail, the multiple stage has been greatly simplified in a majority of the plays that employed it in the sixteenth century.

CONCLUSION

In spite of the limited material available, the present study has yielded a few definite and significant facts concerning the Spanish multiple stage:

1) The multiple stage constituted an important system of staging. It was the usual, if not the exclusive, method in the fifteenth century. In the sixteenth it was employed by a large number of plays—from forty-two to fifty-one and probably many more.

2) The multiple stage was either vertical or horizontal. It consisted either of two different stage levels for Heaven and Earth or two or more simultaneous locations, sometimes decorated and sometimes bare, on the Earth level. Hell was a very rare setting; and only one play, the Majorcan *Consueta del Juy*, definitely required a stage of three levels, with a visible entrance to Hell below the Earth level. The combination of vertical and horizontal multiple stages was very frequent for performances in the fifteenth century (Valencian Nativity and Assumption plays, *Misteri de Adam y Eva*, Elche Assumption play, and Majorcan piece on the Temptation) and very rare in the sixteenth. Only the Assumption theme, dramatized in three *autos*, and probably Carvajal's *Cortes de la Muerte* continued the elaborate combination of two levels with simultaneous horizontal locations.

3) The three principles of juxtaposition of settings or locations, simultaneity of their presentation, and imaginative foreshortening of space were followed by all these plays. Thus, all of them conformed in their construction and performance to one basic system. Within this system, however, variation in details was considerable. In general, there may be said to have existed well defined and conventional techniques used respectively for plays on the Nativity, the Descent from the Cross, and the Assumption. But for the many other subjects to which the multiple system was applied there was no evident convention for the kind, the number, or the

distribution of settings and locations. These seem to have been determined by the requirements of the theme, usually well established by history, custom, and tradition. A few settings like Heaven and the tomb and the entrance to Limbo may always have looked very much the same in whatever play they appeared. But this is not evident, and is indeed very doubtful, in regard to other elements of stage decoration, particularly those like the temple that were put to quite varied uses.

4) From the early fifteenth to the late sixteenth century the multiple stage underwent a change toward simplification. The settings decreased in number and seem, with the exception of Heaven, to have become relatively simple. Simplification may have been due partly to the extension of multiple staging to theaters other than the church and partly to the presence or appearance on the peninsula of other methods which presented different scenes consecutively. Both factors led to the extension of the multiple system to other than religious subjects and to a consequent mingling of the multiple and the consecutive stage methods in both religious and secular plays.

Until other contemporary and later techniques have been systematically studied, the significance of the multiple stage method in the development of Spanish staging cannot be entirely clear. Nevertheless, some measure of its contribution to the later theater may be suggested. As a system it continued on the *carros* of the *autos sacramentales* in the seventeenth and eighteenth centuries. It was a medieval technique persistently surviving in Spain long after it had given way to rival methods in France and Italy. Multiple staging continues to the present time at Elche and in many another popular religious performance where ancient traditions have persisted. Even in the *corrales* it sometimes appeared in the performance of a *comedia*.

Some of the technical and decorative devices of the multiple stage were followed in the secular theaters. Among these may be included the sub-stage level, aerial machinery, the back-stage, and perhaps some particular properties and settings. Although none of these features is an exclusive possession of the multiple stage, their later popularity may have been due partly to long use in multiple stage performances. The elaborate development of the back-stage in the seventeenth century, however, more broadly illustrates a possible general influence of the multiple stage. The back-stage was relatively infrequent, and only occasionally a part of the method. It was confined to those occasions when the desired effect on the audience was one of shock or surprise or wonder and awe. But this motive only partly explains the frequent or regular use of the back-stage in the seventeenth century theaters. Plays in which interest was maintained through an original plot, a complicated intrigue and heroic or comic dialogue in appropriate verse did not need a multiple stage. They did not depend on the spectacle and panorama that of necessity made old, well known subjects seem thrilling and new. They could be presented on small platforms with little or no decoration. But at times it was necessary to change the place of action or to elaborate the stage setting. Then it was that the seventeenth century dramatist used the back-stage. In so doing he obtained either a temporary multiple stage or the benefits that simultaneous staging would have provided naturally. Thus, the back-stage made possible a compromise between the old methods, from which the dramatist could not entirely free himself, and the system of consecutive settings which was eventually to come into general use and continue to the present day.

In its reluctance to yield to new fashions the multiple stage well reflects a fundamental characteristic of Spain and her art. Its persistent medievalism is one of countless manifestations of Spain's tenacious adherence to the traditional, the customary, the popular. Spain could scarcely claim the multiple stage as an innovation or contribution of her own to staging methods; yet the multiple stage became as much a part of Spanish art as did Gothic architecture, many of whose most luxuriant Spanish flowers bloomed after the rest of Europe had turned to newer ideals. Witness Salamanca's *catedral nueva*—a Gothic glory begun in the sixteenth century in Spain's most Renaissance city. In the polyptychs of her many matchless *retablos,* which themselves frequently suggest simultaneous settings, Spain long preserved the ideal of the medieval *Summa.* Garcilaso, Fray Luis and other exquisite voices were heard in a century which was still living and reliving the epic and chivalric exploits of the past in innumerable ballads and romances.[1] And finally, quite like the persistence of the multiple stage was the slow yielding of polyphonic music to the newer forms of modern harmony. Thus was the career of the multiple stage in Spain during the European Renaissance paralleled in the other arts and may serve, with them, as a touchstone of the national genius, the Spanish temper. Perhaps better than the others the art of the theater, since it is the most subject to popular taste and approval, will continue to show the prolongation of old ideals, old forms and old methods in the periods which lie beyond the scope of this study.

[1] Of the Spanish translation of Plautus' *Amphitruo* by the humanist Francisco López de Villalobos, Valbuena says, "precisamente una obra que, por tener a la vez personajes elevados y humildes, no era el típico patrón clásico de la comedia. Señalo esto para advertir cómo hasta los humanistas se sentían atraídos por *el reino de lo múltiple y lo diverso (1515)*" (pp. 80-81; italics mine).

BIBLIOGRAPHY

This bibliographical list includes (1) the works, exclusive of dramatic texts, cited in the present study and (2) a number of other studies (marked with an asterisk—*) dealing either primarily or only incidentally with Spanish staging prior to the seventeenth century. It is the author's hope that this list, however imperfect and tentative, may be of some service in other investigations of early staging.

Alcahalí [y Mosquera], D. José [María]' Ruiz de Lihory y Pardines Barón de, *La música en Valencia,* Valencia, 1903.

Alenda y Mira, Jenaro, *Relaciones de solemnidades y fiestas públicas de España,* Madrid, 1903, I (only Vol. pub.).

————"Catálogo de autos sacramentales, historiales y alegóricos," in *BRAE,* III (1916)—X (1923).

Alfonso el Sabio, *Las Siete Partidas,* Madrid, 1807.

Alonso Cortés, N., *El teatro en Valladolid,* Madrid, 1923.

Alvarez Gamero, Santiago, "Las fiestas de Toledo en 1555," in *RHi,* XXXI (1914), 392-485.

Álvarez de la Villa, Alfredo, *Juan del Enzina. El Aucto del Repelón,* Paris, [n.d.].

Ancona, Alessandro d', *Origini del teatro italiano,* 2ª ed., Torino, 1891, 2 Vols.

Arco, Ricardo del, "Misterios, autos sacramentales y otras fiestas en la catedral de Huesca," in *RABM,* XLI (1920), 263-274.

* Atkinson, William, "Hernán Pérez de Oliva, Teatro," in *RHi,* LXIX (1927), 521 ff.

Baist, Gottfried, *Die spanische Literatur,* in Gustav Gröber, *Grundriss der romanischen Philologie,* II, ii, Strassburg, 1897, 383 ff.

Bapst, Germain, *Essai sur l'histoire du théâtre,* Paris, 1893.

Barbieri, Francisco Asenjo, see Cañete.

Bonnell, John K., "The Easter *Sepulchrum* in its Relation to the Architecture of the High Altar," in *PMLA,* XXXI (1916), 664-712.

Bonilla y San Martín, Adolfo, "Cinco obras dramáticas anteriores a Lope de Vega," in *RHi,* XXVII (1912), 390-496.

———— *Las bacantes o del origen del teatro,* Madrid, 1921.

Brooks, Neil C., *The Sepulchre of Christ in Art and Liturgy with special reference to the Liturgic Drama,* in University of Illinois Studies in Language and Literature, VII (1921), Num. 2, 139-250.

———— "The 'Sepulchrum Christi,'" in *JEGP,* XXVII (1928), 147-161.

Buchanan, Milton A., "At a Spanish Theater in the Seventeenth Century" (A Summary of a paper read before the Modern Language Club, University College, on January 27, 1908), in *The University Monthly,* published by University of Toronto Alumni Assoc., April, 1908, 204-209; May, 1908, 230-236.

Calvert, Albert F., *The Escorial,* London and New York, 1907.

—— *Sculpture in Spain,* London and New York, 1912.

Cañete, Manuel, *Farsas y Églogas al modo y estilo pastoril y castellano fechas por Lucas Fernández, salmantino,* Madrid, 1867.

—— *Tragedia llamada Josefina sacada de la profundidad de la Sagrada Escriptura y trobada por Micael de Carvajal de la ciudad de Placencia,* Madrid, 1870 (Sociedad de bibliófilos españoles, 6).

—— *Teatro español del siglo XVI,* Madrid, 1885.

—— and Barbieri, Francisco Asenjo, *Teatro completo de Juan del Encina,* Madrid, 1893.

Cervantes Saavedra, Miguel de, *Comedias y entremeses,* Madrid, 1615, "Prólogo al lector," pub. by Rodolfo Schevill and Adolfo Bonilla, Madrid, 1915.

—— *El ingenioso hidalgo Don Quijote de la Mancha,* Madrid, 1615, II, 11.

Chambers, E. K., The Mediaeval Stage, Oxford, 1903, 2 Vols.

—— The Elizabethan Stage, Oxford, 1923, 4 Vols.

Cobarruuias Orozco, Sebastián de, *Tesoro de la lengua castellana, o española,* Madrid, 1611.

Cohen, Gustave, *Histoire de la mise en scène dans le théâtre religieux français du moyen age,* nouvelle ed., revue et augmentée, Paris, 1926.

Corbató, Hermenegildo, "Notas sobre *El Misterio de Elche* y otros dramas sagrados de Valencia," in *Hispania,* XV (1932), 103-108.

—— *Los Misterios del Corpus de Valencia,* Berkeley, Calif., 1932.

Cotarelo y Mori, Emilio, *Juan del Encina y los orígenes del teatro español,* Madrid, 1901.

*—— "El primer auto sacramental del teatro español y noticia de su autor El Bachiller Hernan López de Yanguas," in *RABM,* VII (1902). 251-272.

*—— *Bibliografía de las controversias sobre la licitud del teatro en España,* Madrid, 1904.

—— *Obras de Lope de Rueda,* Madrid, 1908, I, "Prólogo."

*—— *Cancionero de Juan del Encina, 1ª ed., 1496.* Publicado en facsímile por la Real Academia Española, Madrid, 1928.

*—— *Farsas y Églogas por Lucas Fernández,* reproducción en facsímile de la 1ª ed. de 1514 publícala la Real Academia Española, Madrid, 1929.

*—— "Ensayo histórico sobre la zarzuela o sea el drama lírico español desde su origen a fines del siglo XIX," in *BRAE,* XIX (1932)—.

* Cotarelo y Valledor, Armando, *El teatro de Cervantes,* Madrid, 1915.

Crawford, J. P. Wickersham, *"Representacion de los mártires Justo y Pastor*, de Francisco de las Cuebas," in *RHi*, XIX (1908), 428 ff.

—— "The Devil as a Dramatic Figure in the Spanish Religious Drama before Lope de Vega," in *RR*, I (1910), 302-312, 374-383.

—— "The Catalan *Mascarón* and an episode in Jacob van Maerlant's *Merlijn*," in *PMLA*, XXVI (1911), 31-50.

—— "The Pastor and Bobo in the Spanish Religious Drama of the Sixteenth Century," in *RR*, II (1911), 376-401.

—— "Comedia á lo pastoril para la noche de navidad," in *RHi*, XXIV (1911), 497-541.

—— "Auto de la Quinta Angustia que Nuestra Señora Passo al Pie de la Cruz," in *RR*, III (1912), 280.

* —— "Notes on the *Amphitrion* and *Los Menemnos* of Juan de Timoneda," in *MLR*, IX (1914), 248-251.

—— *The Spanish Pastoral Drama*, Philadelphia, 1915.

—— "A Sixteenth-Century Spanish Analogue of *Measure for Measure*," in *MLN*, XXXV (1920), 330-335.

—— "A Note on the Boy Bishop in Spain," in *RR*, XII (1921).

—— *Spanish Drama before Lope de Vega*, Philadelphia, 1922.

Creizenach, Wilhelm, *Geschichte des neueren Dramas*, 2d ed., Halle, a.S., I, 1911; II, 1918; III, 1923.

Crónica del Condestable Miguel Lucas de Iranzo, in *Memorial histórico español*, VIII, Madrid, 1855.

* Díaz de Escovar, Narciso, *El Teatro en Málaga. Apuntes históricos de los siglos XVI, XVII, XVIII*, Málaga, 1896.

—— *Anales del teatro español anteriores al año 1550*, Madrid, 1910.

—— *Anales de la escena española correspondientes a los años 1551 a 1580*, Madrid, 1910.

Du Méril [Edelestand Pontas], *Les origines latines du théâtre moderne*, Leipzig and Paris, 1897.

Durán i Sanpere, Agustí, "Un misteri de la Passió a Cervera," in *Estudis universitaris catalans*, VII (1913), 241 ff.

España sagrada, Vol. 45, Madrid, 1832.

Fernández Duro, Cesáreo, "Apuntes para la historia del teatro," in *La Ilustración Española y Americana*, Madrid, 1883, Num. XXXIX, 234-235, 315-318, 350-351.

Fischel, Oskar, "Art and the Theatre," in *The Burlington Magazine*, LXVI (1935), 4-14, 54-67.

Foulché-Delbosc, Isabel, and Puyol, Julio, "Bibliografía de R. Foulché-Delbosc, in *RHi*, LXXX¹ (1933), 85-192.

Foulché-Delbosc, R., "Madame d'Aulnoy et l'Espagne," in *RHi*, LXVII (1926), 1 ff.

Frank, Grace, "Popular Iconography of the Passion," in *PMLA,* XLVI (1931), 333-340.

Gallardo, Bartolomé José, *Ensayo de una biblioteca española de libros raros y curiosos,* ed. M. R. Zarco del Valle and J. Sancho Rayón, Madrid, 1863-1889, 4 Vols.

García Içazbalceta, Joaquín, *Coloquios espirituales y sacramentales y poesías sagradas del presbítero Fernán González de Eslava (escritor del siglo XVI),* 2ª ed., conforme a la primera hecha en México en 1610, México, 1877.

García, López, Juan Catalina, *Ensayo de una tipografía complutense,* Madrid, 1889.

García Silvestre, Manuel, *Historia sumaria de la literatura catalana,* Barcelona, 1932.

García Soriano, Justo, "El teatro de colegio en España. Noticia y examen de algunas de sus obras," in *BRAE,* XIV (1927)—.

* Gillet, Joseph E., "La aparición que hizo Jesu Christo a los dos discípulos que yvan a Emaus: an Early Sixteenth-Century Play," in *RR,* XIII (1922), 228-251.

—— "Esteban Martín (*or* Martínez) : Auto, como San Juan fue concebido (1528)," in *RR,* XVII (1926), 41-64.

—— "Perolópez Ranjel, Farça a Honor & Reuerencia del glorioso nascimiento (Early Sixteenth Century)," in *PMLA,* XLI (1926), 860-890.

—— "Danza del Santíssimo Nacimiento, a Sixteenth Century Play by Pedro Suárez de Robles," in *PMLA,* XLIII (1928), 614-634.

—— "Torres Naharro and the Spanish Drama of the Sixteenth Century," in *Estudios eruditos in Memoriam de Adolfo Bonilla y San Martín,* II, Madrid, 1930.

—— *Micael de Carvajal. Tragedia Josephina,* in *Elliott Monographs,* Num. 28, Princeton and Paris, 1932.

—— "Timoneda's (?) *Aucto. de la Quinta Angustia,*" in MLN, XLVII (1932), 7-8.

—— "Tres Pasos de la Pasión y una Égloga de la Resurrección (Burgos, 1520)," in *PMLA,* XLVII (1932), 949-980.

—— "An Easter-play by Juan de Pedraza (1549)," in *RHi,* LXXXI¹ (1933), 550-607.

—— and Williams, Edwin B., "Tragedia de los amores de Eneas y de la Reyna Dido," in *PMLA,* XLVI (1931), 353-431.

Gómez-Moreno, Manuel, *Provincia de León,* [II], [Madrid], 1926.

González, P. Raimundo, "El teatro religioso en la edad media. Los Misterios cíclicos," in *CD,* CXV-CXXIII.

González Pedroso, Eduardo, *Autos sacramentales desde su origen hasta fines del siglo XVII (BAE*, LVIII), Madrid, 1865, "Prólogo del colector," vii-lxi.

* Gonzalez de Salas, Don Ivsepe Antonio, *Nueva Idea de la Tragedia Antigva, o Ilvstracion Vltima al libro singvlar de Poetica de Aristoteles stagirita,* 2 Partes, Madrid, 1778. (1st ed., 1633).

* Gual, Adrián, *Temas de historia del teatro,* Vol. I of Publicaciones del instituto del teatro nacional, Barcelona, 1929.

Holbein's Icones Historiarvm Veteris Testamenti, a photo-lith facsimile reprint from the Lyons edition of 1547, ed. Henry Green, M.A., Manchester and London, 1869.

House, Ralph E., "A Study of Encina and the Égloga Interlocutoria," in *RR*, VII (1916), 458-469.

* Icaza, F. A. de, "Cristóbal de Llerena y los orígenes del teatro en la América española," in *RFE*, VIII (1921), 121-130.

Illustration l', Sept. 18, 1897. "La fête de l' Assomption à Elche."

* Jack, William Shaffer, *The Early Entremés in Spain; The Rise of a Dramatic Form,* Philadelphia, 1923.

Johnson, Mildred Edith, *The "Aucto del Castillo de Emaus" and the "Aucto de la Iglesia" of Juan Timoneda,* University of Iowa Studies in Spanish Language and Literature, Num. 4, Iowa City, 1933.

Juliá, Eduard, *Régles de Amor i Parlament de un Hom i una Fembra.* Obra atribuida al canceller Mossen Domingo Mascó segle XIV, [Castelló, 1926].

* Juliá Martínez, Eduardo, *Poetas dramáticos valencianos,* Madrid, 1929, I, v-cxxxv (Observaciones preliminares).

——— "Representaciones teatrales de carácter popular en la provincia de Castellón," in *BRAE*, XVII (1930), 97-112.

Jusserand, J. J., "A Note on Pageants and 'Scaffolds Hye,' " in *An English Miscellany presented by Dr. [Frederick James] Furnivall in honour of his seventy-fifth birthday.* Oxford, 1901, 183-195.

* King, Georgiana Goddard, *The Play of the Sibyl Cassandra,* Bryn Mawr, New York, 1921.

Kohler, Dr. Eugen, *Sieben spanische dramatische Eklogen,* Dresden, 1911 (Gesellschaft für romanische Literatur, 27).

Laborde, Le Comte A. de, *La bible moralisée illustrée,* I, Paris, 1911.

* Lamarca, D. Luis, *El teatro de Valencia desde su origen hasta nuestros días,* Valencia, 1840.

Lampérez y Romea, Vicente, *Historia de la arquitectura cristiana española en la edad media,* 2ª ed., Madrid, 1930, II.

Latorre y Badillo, M., "Representación de los autos sacramentales," in *RABM,* XXV (1911), 189-211, 342-367; XXVI (1912), 72-89, 236-262.

132   THE MULTIPLE STAGE IN SPAIN

Lawrence, W. J., "Windows on the Pre-Restoration Stage," in *Anglia*, XXXVI, neue folge Band XXIV (1912), 450-478.

Lefort, Paul, *La peinture espagnole*, Paris, [1893].

Lopez Pinciano, Alonso, *Philosophia antigva poetica*, Madrid, 1596.

López Prudencio, J., *Diego Sánchez de Badajoz. Estudio crítico, biográfico y bibliográfico*, Madrid, 1915.

Llabrés, Gabriel, "Un hallazgo literario interesante," in *BSAL*, 10 abril de 1887, pp. 53 ff.

——— "Repertorio de 'Consuetas' representadas en las iglesias de Mallorca (siglos XV y XVI)," in *RABM*, V (1901), 920-927.

Mâle, Émile, *L'art religieux de la fin du moyen âge en France*, 3ᵉ ed., Paris, 1925.

Mal Lara, Juan de, *Recebimiento que hizo la Ciudad de Sevilla al Rey D. Phelipe II*, [En Sevilla, en casa de Alonso Escriuano, 1570]. Reproducción fotolitográfica by the Bibliófilos Andaluces, Sevilla, 1878.

Mantzius, Karl, *A History of Theatrical Art in Ancient and Modern Times*, authorized translation by Louise von Cossel, II, London, 1903.

* Mariana, Juan de, *Tratado contra los juegos públicos*, in *Obras (BAE, XXXI)*, Madrid, 1854, 413-462.

Mariscal de Gante, Jaime, *Los autos sacramentales desde sus orígenes hasta mediados del siglo XVIII*, Madrid, 1911.

Mascarón, pub. by Próspero de Bofarull y Mascaró, in *Documentos literarios en antigua lengua catalana (siglos XIV y XV)*, Barcelona, 1857 (*Colección de documentos inéditos del archivo general de la corona de Aragón*, XIII), 107-117.

Mayer, August L., *Die sevillaner Malerschule*, Leipzig, 1911.

——— *Geschichte der spanischen Malerei*, Leipzig, 1913.

——— *Spanische Barock-Plastik*, München, 1923.

Menéndez y Pelayo, Marcelino, *Antología de poetas líricos castellanos*, VI, Madrid, 1896.

——— *Tres comedias de Alonso de la Vega*, Dresden, 1905 (Gesellschaft für romanische literatur, VI).

Meredith, Joseph A., *Introito and Loa in the Spanish Drama of the Sixteenth Century*, in series in Romanic Languages and Literatures of the University of Pennsylvania, Num. 16, Philadelphia, 1928.

Mérimée, Henri, *L'art dramatique à Valencia depuis les origines jusqu'au commencement du XVIIᵉ siècle*, Toulouse, 1913.

* ——— *Spectacles et comédiens à Valencia (1580-1630)*, Toulouse and Paris, 1913.

Michaëlis de Vasconcellos, Carolina, *Autos portugueses de Gil Vicente y de la escuela vicentina*, ed. facs., Madrid, 1922.

Milá y Fontanals, Manuel, *Obras completas*, coleccionadas por el Dr. D. Marcelino Menéndez y Pelayo, VI, Barcelona, 1895, 203-379 (*Orígenes del teatro catalán*).

* Milego, Julio, *El teatro en Toledo durante los siglos XVI y XVII*, Valencia, 1909.

Morales, Ambrosio de, *La vida, el martyrio, la inuencion, las grandezas, y las translaciones de los gloriosos niños Martyres san Justo y Pastor, y el solenne triumpho con que fueron recebidas sus santas Reliquias en Alcalá de Henares en su postrera translacion*. En Alcala en casa de Andres de Angulo, 1568.

Moratín, Leandro Fernández de, *Orígenes del teatro español*, in *Obras*, I, Madrid, 1830; also in *BAE*, II, Madrid, 1846.

Morel-Fatio, Alfred, "La *Farsa llamada Salamantina* de Bartolomé Palau," in *BHi*, II (1900), 237-304.

Muñoz Morillejo, Joaquín, *Escenografía española*, Madrid, 1923.

* Niessen, Carl, *Das Bühnenbild. Ein Kulturgeschichtlicheratlas*, I and II, Bonn, 1924; III, IV and V, Bonn, 1927.

Norris, Edwin, *The Ancient Cornish Drama*, Oxford, 1859, 2 vols.

Parker, Alexander A., "Notes on the Religious Drama in Medieval Spain and the Origins of the 'Auto Sacramental,'" in *MLR*, XXX (1935), 170-182.

Paz y Mélia, A., *Sales españolas*, II, Madrid, 1902.

Pedrell, Felipe, *La festa d'Elche, ou Le drama lyrique liturgique espagnol. Le trépas et l'assomption de la Vierge*, Paris, 1906 (ext. des Sammelbände der internationalen Musikgesellschaft, Leipzig, Jan.-March, 1901, 203-252).

Pellicer, Casiano, *Tratado histórico sobre el origen y progresos de la comedia y del histrionismo en España*, Madrid, 1804.

Penn, Dorothy, *The Staging of the "Miracles de Nostre Dame par personnages" of the ms. Cangé*, New York [1933]. (Publication of the Institute of French Studies).

Pérez Pastor, Cristóbal, *Nuevos datos acerca del histrionismo español en los siglos XVI y XVII*, Madrid, 1901.

────── 2ª serie, publicada con un índice por Georges Cirot, Bordeaux, 1914 (reprinted from *BHi*, 1906-1914).

Petit de Julleville, Louis, *Histoire du théâtre en France; les mystères*, Paris, 1880, 2 Vols.

* Pfandl, Ludwig, *Spanische Kultur und Sitte des 16. und 17. Jahrhunderts. Eine Einführung in die Blütezeit der spanischen Literatur und Kunst* [München], 1924; translated into Spanish with a prologue by P. Félix García agustino, Barcelona, [1929].

Pie, Joan, "Autos sagramentals del sigle XIV," in *Revista de la Asociación artístico-arqueológica Barcelonesa*, 1893 (año 2º).

Pinheiro da Veiga, Tomé, *Fastiginia o Fastos Geniales*, translated into Spanish by Narciso Alonso Cortés, Valladolid, 1916.

Pons, Joseph-Sébastien, *La littérature catalane en Rousillon au XVIIᵉ et au XVIIIᵉ siècle*, Toulouse-Paris, 1929.

Pratt, Oscar de, *Gil Vicente, notas e comentários*, Lisboa, 1931.

Puyol, Julio, see Foulché-Delbosc, Isabel.

* Ramírez de Arellano, Rafael, *El teatro en Córdoba*, Ciudad-Real, 1912.

Ratcliff, Dillwyn F., "The *Mystery of Elche* in 1931," in *Hispania*, XV (1932), 109-116.

Rennert, Hugo Albert, "The Staging of Lope de Vega's Comedies," in *RHi*, XV (1906), 453-485.

―――― *The Spanish Stage in the time of Lope de Vega*, New York, 1909.

―――― and Castro, Américo, *Vida de Lope de Vega (1562-1635)*, Madrid, 1919.

Restori, A., "Los trabajos de Joseph, auto del licenciado Juan de Caxés," in *RHi*, IX (1902), 355 ff.

Rigal, Eugène, *Le théâtre français avant la période classique (fin du XVIᵉ et commencement du XVIIᵉ siècle)*, Paris, 1901.

Rodríguez, P. Conrado, "El teatro religioso de Gómez Manrique," in *RyC*, XXVIII (1934), 327-342; XXIX (1935), 68-95.

Rojas, Agustín de, *El viaje entretenido*, in *NBAE*, XXI (Vol. 4 of *Orígenes de la novela*, pub. by Adolfo Bonilla y San Martín), 460-614; the *loa de la comedia* is also included in Emilio Cotarelo y Mori, *Colección de entremeses, loas, bailes, jácaras y mojigangas desde fines del siglo XVI á mediados del XVIII*, I, 2, Madrid, 1911 (*NBAE*, XVIII), Num. 92, pp. 347-349.

Rothschild, Nathan James Édouard, baron de, *Le mistère du viel testament*, Paris, III, 1881.

Rouanet, Léo, *Colección de autos, farsas, y coloquios del siglo XVI*, Madrid and Barcelona, 1901, 4 vols.

―――― review of Pedrell, *La 'festa' d'Elche*, in *RHi*, VIII (1901), 540-542.

―――― "Oeuvres dramatiques du licencié Juan Caxes," in *RHi*, VIII (1901), 83 ff.

―――― *Bartolomé Palau: Farsa llamada custodia del hombre*, Paris, 1911.

Rufo, Juan, *Alabanças de la comedia*, in Ferdinand Wolf, *Studien zur Geschichte der spanischen und portugiesischen Nationalliteratur*, Berlin, 1859.

Salvá y Mallén, Pedro, *Catálogo de la biblioteca de Salvá*, Valencia, 1872, 2 vols.

Sánchez-Arjona, José, *Noticias referentes a los anales del teatro en Sevilla desde Lope de Rueda hasta fines del siglo XVII*, Sevilla, 1898.

Sanchis y Sivera, José (Lázaro Floro), *La dramática en nuestra catedral durante la edad media* (De *El Almanaque de Las Provincias*), Valencia, 1908 (part of a chapter of the author's later *La catedral de Valencia*, Valencia, 1909).

Schack, Adolfo Federico conde de, *Historia de la literatura y del arte dramático en España*, trad. directamente del alemán al castellano por Eduardo de Mier, 5 vols., Madrid, 1885-1887.

Schmidt, P. Expeditus, *Die Bühnenverhältnisse des deutschen Schuldramas und seiner volkstümlichen Ableger im sechzehnten Jahrhundert*, Berlin, 1903 (Forschungen zur neuren Literaturgeschichte herausgegeben von Dr. Franz Muncker, XXIV).

* —— *El auto sacramental y su importancia en el arte escénico de la época*, conferencia dada el 11 de noviembre de 1927, Madrid, 1930 (Conferencias dadas en el centro de intercambio intelectual germano-español, XXV).

* Sepúlveda, Ricardo, *El corral de la Pachea*, Madrid, 1888.

Serrano Cañete, Joaquín, *El Misterio de Adam y Eva*, Valencia, [1899].

Shoemaker, William H., "Windows on the Spanish Stage in the Sixteenth Century," in *HR*, II (1934), 308-318.

Spencer, Hazelton, "How Shakespeare Staged his plays: some notes on the Dubiety on non-textual evidence," in *The Johns Hopkins Alumni Magazine*, XX (1932).

Stuart, Donald Clive, *Stage Decoration in France in the Middle Ages*, New York, 1910.

—— "The Stage Setting of Hell and the Iconography of the Middle Ages, in *RR*, IV (1913), 330-342.

* Subirá, José, *La participación musical en el antiguo teatro español*, Barcelona, 1930.

Thorndike, Ashley H., *Shakespeare's Theater*, New York, 1916.

Ticknor, George, *History of Spanish Literature*, 3d American ed., Boston, 1866, 3 vols.

* Trend, J. B., "Escenografía madrileña en el siglo XVII," in *RevBAM*, III (1926), 269-281.

* [Uhagón y Guardamino, Francisco Rafael de, marqués de Laurencín], *Relaciones históricas de los siglos XVI y XVII*, Madrid, 1896 (Sociedad de bibliófilos españoles, 32).

Valbuena, Angel, *Literatura dramática española*, Barcelona and Buenos Aires, Editorial Labor, [1930].

Valera, Juan, *Juanita la Larga*, Madrid, 1896, Capítulo XXXVI.

* Vidal Pierre, "Mélanges d'histoire, de littérature et de philologie catalane," in *Rev. des langues romanes*, XXXII (1888), 333-359; XXXIII
(1889), 84-100.

[Villanueva, Jaime], *Viage literario á las iglesias de España*, pub. by Joaquín
Lorenzo Villanueva, Madrid and Valencia, 1803-1852, 22 vols.

Walberg, E., *Juan de la Cueva et son "Exemplar Poético,"* Lund, 1904.

Weise, Georg, *Spanische Plastik aus sieben Jahrhunderten*, Reutlingen,
Band II (Abbildungen), 1927.

Whyte, Florence, "Three autos of Jorge de Montemayor," in *PMLA*,
XLIII (1928), 953-989.

Williams, E. B., see Gillet.

Williams, Ronald Boal, *The Staging of Plays in the Spanish Peninsula
Prior to 1555*, University of Iowa Studies in Spanish Language and
Literature, Num. 5, Iowa City, 1935.

Young, Karl, "Officium Pastorum: A Study of the Dramatic Developments
within the Liturgy of Christmas," in *Transactions of the Wisconsin
Academy of Sciences, Arts, and Letters*, XVII[1] (1914), 299-396.

―――― *The Drama of the Medieval Church*, Oxford, 1933, 2 vols.

INDEX OF PLAYS

Reference to plays marked with an asterisk (*) is made by title only.

INDEX OF SUBJECTS AND PROPER NAMES

The names of authors of plays will be found also in
the INDEX OF PLAYS in connection with
their dramatic works

143

grain, see wheat field
grating, 80, 88; *rella*, 19, 38
grave, 53, 56, 57, 58, 71 n. 23, 103, 105, 119

hammer, 71 n. 21 (*martillos*), 75
head, 49, 92 (human)
Heaven, 12-15, 17, 23, 25, 27, 28, 29, 30, 31, 33-38, 40-48, 49, 58-59, 82, 117, 118 (*nube*), 123, 124 (*vueltas*), 13 (*girando*), 45, 46, 47; see also levels
Hell, 8, 12, 21-23, 24-26, 27, 28, 37, 48-53, 57-59, 123; cave (*cueva*), 48, 52; entrance, 48, 49-52, 53, 57, 58, 59, 123; interior invisible, 48, 50, 51, 52, 53 n. 46, 57, 58, 59; medieval fortress, 48 n. 28; mouth (*boca*), 49, 50, 51, 52, 58, 59, 77, 78; off stage, 48-49, 51, 52, 57, 59; tortures, 22, 59 n. 61; see also levels, Limbo
hermitage, 80, 81, 85, 102 n. 119, 104, 110, 111 n. 143
hiding place, 23 (Hell), 24, 29, 30, 36, 55, 104, 106
hill, 41, 72
Holy City, 31, 38, 120
honey, 85
horatori, see chapel
Horozco, Sebastián de, 74 n. 29
house (home), 78, 79, 80, 81, 89 n. 69, 94, 95 n. 88 (hut), 103, 104, 106, 108, 111 n. 143, 114, 119; *casa, cambra*, etc. of the Virgin, 21-24, 25, 26, 28-30, 33, 38, 99, 101; *posada*, 76, 79, 81; *estancia*, 102 n. 119; *casa colgada*, 85, 119
huerta de Doña Elvira, 56
huerto, 33
Huesca, 44 n. 19, 49
humanists, 126 n. 1

iconography, 3-5, 25, 34 n. 77, 55 n. 48, 69 n. 19, 72, 81 n. 45, 92 n. 76, 112; see also painting, sculpture, wood cut, sketch
iglesia, see theater
image, 29, 31 (*en figura*), 33, 34, 70, 99, 119; see also statue, doll
imagination, see spectator
Indies, 31 n. 70, 42 n. 7
infierno(s), infern, etc., see Hell, Limbo
inn, 80, 81, 90; *venta*, 80, 81; *mesón*, 90, 91

introito, 6
Iranzo, Condestable, Miguel Lucas de, 12, 15
Isabel la Católica, 13
Italy, 124; see also setting, Italian

Jaen, 15, 20 n. 32, 36, 37, 38, 49
jail (prison, *cárcel*, etc.), 62, 63, 64, 79, 80, 81, 92, 93, 102 n. 119
Jerusalem, 8, 18, 44 n. 17 (Hierusalem), 101, 104, 106, 107
Jesuit, 63, 64 n. 16
jewel, 80 (*cadenas de oro*); see also *joyería*
Jonas play, 112 n. 146
joyería, 80 (jewelry shop)
juegos de escarnio, 11
jug, 55
Juliá, Eduardo, 11 n. 5

knocker, 28, 38
Kohler, 71 n. 23
Künselsau, 117

ladder, 67, 68, 70, 71, 75, 80
Latin plays, see liturgical drama
lectern, 83
León, Fray Luis de, 126
letrillas, 13 n. 11
levels (stage), 10, 12, 14, 17, 25, 36, 40-59, 79; lower, 24, 25, 34, 36-37, 45 n. 20, 49 n. 34, 52-59; sub-stage, 53-59, 103, 124; three, 52, 59, 91 n. 71, 123; upper, 27, 34, 35-36, 40-48, 58, 59, 123
Leviathan, 49, 50, 51, 58
leyte, 92 n. 77
Libre de obres, 15 n. 17, 31 n. 69
Liège, Hubert Thomas of, 50
lienzo, 14, 31, 45, 47, 63; see also cloth, colored, and sheet
light, 22 n. 42 (*ciris*), 68 (*luz*), 94 (*candiles*); see also fire
Limbo, 48 n. 28, 86-88, 98, 105, 113, 114, 119, 124; *infierno(s)*, 87, 88, 89
Limoges, 20 n. 32
linterna, 29 n. 64
lion, 56
liturgical drama, 8, 21 n. 2, 62, 73 n. 27, 81 n. 48, 95 n. 87, 96
loa, 6
location: defined, 10; number, *passim*, esp. 118, 123; see also settings, consecutive

VITA

I, William Hutchinson Shoemaker, was born on March 2, 1902, at Norristown, Pennsylvania, the son of Edward Conard and Margaret Walker Shoemaker. I received my primary and secondary education in the Norristown public schools and in George School, Bucks County, Pennsylvania, from which I was graduated in 1920. Four years later I was graduated from Princeton University with the degree of Bachelor of Arts. After teaching Spanish for two years at Lake Forest Academy, Lake Forest, Illinois, I returned to Princeton as instructor and graduate student in the Department of Modern Languages. In 1928 I received the degree of Master of Arts. I have studied under Professors C. C. Marden, E. C. Armstrong, F. C. Tarr, D. L. Buffum, P. A. Chapman, and J. E. Gillet.